# Feet to the Fire

# Feet to the Fire

## How to Exemplify and Create the Accountability That Creates Great Companies

Lorraine A. Moore

*Feet to the Fire: How to Exemplify and Create the Accountability that Creates Great Companies*
Copyright © Business Expert Press, LLC, 2017.

All rights reserved. No part of this publication may be reproduced, stored in a retrieval system, or transmitted in any form or by any means—electronic, mechanical, photocopy, recording, or any other except for brief quotations, not to exceed 250 words, without the prior permission of the publisher.

First published in 2017 by
Business Expert Press, LLC
222 East 46th Street, New York, NY 10017
www.businessexpertpress.com

ISBN-13: 978-1-63157-519-8 (print)
ISBN-13: 978-1-63157-520-4 (e-book)

Business Expert Press Human Resource Management and Organizational Behavior Collection

Collection ISSN: 1946-5637 (print)
Collection ISSN: 1946-5645 (electronic)

Cover and interior design by S4Carlisle Publishing Services Private Ltd., Chennai, India

First edition: 2017

10 9 8 7 6 5 4 3 2 1

Printed in the United States of America

## Abstract

Today's global, transparent, and often-turbulent economy requires a new world order in leadership. The business environment has forever changed, and leaders have been caught flat-footed. Our heroes and heroines are hard to find. Many experienced leaders and certainly newer leaders are ill prepared for the imposing regulatory environment and community activism that permeates oil and gas/energy, health care, financial services, pharmaceuticals, and more. Talented, passionate, and committed people will change the world—for their customers, their colleagues, their shareholders, and their employees. However, to unleash people's potential, to generate recurring revenue growth, foster innovation, and maximize productivity, we need to hold each other's feet to the fire. We need to create a culture of accountability. What are the benefits of an accountable organization? They are numerous. Increased employee engagement, higher ROI on projects, retention of your best performers, improved customer loyalty; greater innovation and increased profitability all result from higher levels of accountability.

## Keywords

accountability, career, career advice, CEO, consulting, Enbridge, executive performance, executive presence, implementation, innovation, leadership, leadership courage, leading in difficult times, leading others, mergers and acquisitions, performance, performance improvement, performance under pressure, self-awareness, strategic, strategy, succession, talent, talent management, TD

# Advanced Quotes for *Feet to the Fire*

"*Feet to the Fire* is the perfect read for any leader who is looking to build a more effective and meaningful leadership approach. Leaders at any level can learn something from Lorraine's coaching skills. Her expertise on in-spiring and guiding others, executing core principles and leading more effectively is beneficial for all executives. *Feet to the Fire* reinforces the importance of innovation when forging our way through a challenging economic climate."

—Richard Scott
*President and CEO, All Weather Windows*

"Lorraine Moore's book is a must read for both novice and experienced leaders who are looking for sophisticated practical information on how to lead powerfully. Unlike most books on leadership, *Feet to the Fire* does not provide a simple step-by-step "formula" for success but, instead, offers insightful information and suggestions for how leaders might think and behave more complexly. Informed by her many years of experience in leadership positions and her work with successful leaders Moore offers both pragmatic information and insightful analyses. *Feet to the Fire* has affirmed many things that I know are important in cultivating effective leadership and it also challenged some of my assumptions and habits of practice. This is the hallmark of a book that truly educates."

—Dennis Sumara, PhD
*Professor and Dean, Werkliund School of EducationUniversity of Calgary*

"Lorraine Moore is an insightful leader and executive coach who brings a wealth of knowledge to the table in *Feet to the Fire*. Her years of experience as a senior executive, mentor to CEO's and leader of CEO Forums come alive in this important work that shares her insights and shared learning from a cross section of industries and industry leaders. Lorraine challenges leaders to hold themselves and their teams accountable both professionally and personally in the context of the ever elusive work life balance that is so frequently ill defined. I have found her impartial, thought provoking counsel to be an invaluable game changer."

—David Blodgett
*President & Chief Executive Officer*

# Contents

*Foreword* ................................................................................ *xi*
*Acknowledgements* ............................................................ *xiii*
*Introduction* ......................................................................... *xv*

Chapter 1  Creating a Culture of Accountability ........................... 1
Chapter 2  Establishing a Career without Sacrificing a Life ........ 7
Chapter 3  Constructing Your Leadership Brand ...................... 27
Chapter 4  Excelling at Career Turning Points ......................... 51
Chapter 5  Multifaceted Leadership .......................................... 73
Chapter 6  Harnessing Performance .......................................... 87
Chapter 7  Talent for the Twenty-First Century ..................... 101
Chapter 8  Elevating Others to Soar: Leading Organizational Change ..................................................................... 115
Chapter 9  Elevating Results through Innovation .................. 131

*Index* ................................................................................. *145*

# Foreword

Working with Fortune 500 firms globally, I often encountered the metaphors "burning platform" and "straw man." The former was meant to suggest that people would move if you set the floor on fire, and the latter that it was useful to create a simulacrum before committing to the actual movement of, and communication with, people.

I found these to be colorful metaphors but superficial actions, clever in the conference room, and ineffective in reality. I finally chided one senior executive group by pointing out that in that very room they needed straw men on a burning platform—move or be consumed by change.

Ironically, the facile kids' game "follow the leader" has morphed into a management philosophy. People in organizational life do not believe what they read or hear, but only believe what they see. In the kids' game, the point was to lose your followers by choosing tough paths; in the management game the point is to enable the followers to successfully follow and support you. Yet, too often, it is the kids' game result that occurs, with the followers advertently or inadvertently losing their leader's path.

Lorraine Moore has been on both sides of the boardroom door, as an executive and as a consultant. What she has created in *Feet to the Fire* is a brilliant path toward real accountability, self-created, and perpetuated. This is not a mindless burning platform or an inane dance barefoot across hot coals. Nor is it a hypothetical straw man.

This is the real deal for the accountability that not only retains followers but also motivates them to achieve great performance.

We have created iconic leaders in our business environment and we have condemned notorious ones. But my observation over thirty years of consulting is that it is the everyday actions and behaviors of executives that stimulate commitment over compliance and dedication over dereliction. *Feet to the Fire* is the story of sustainable innovation, appealing brand, practical leadership, and spectacular results to which any leader can aspire, and toward which every leader should be marching—followed successfully by talented people.

This is a career-building and a life-changing approach, and only someone with Lorraine Moore's unique background and bold insights can make it so simple and possible. Like every star consultant, she make things clear, not complex, and pragmatic, not theoretical.

Great entities—companies, schools, governments, teams, even nations—move forward when they unite behind a leader's values which are mutually attractive. Great leaders understand this. They do not try to lose people, they try to retain them. They do not set fire to the room, they set fire to creativity, performance, and the accomplishment of goals.

Enjoy *Feet to the Fire* which will stimulate you and your organization never to be content on any platform, but to constantly seek new standards and new journeys.

Alan Weiss, PhD
Author, *Million Dollar Consulting,*
*Million Dollar Maverick*
and over sixty other books

# Acknowledgments

It takes a village to conceive a book. Throughout my corporate career, I learned much from my bosses and my employees. Now, my clients are a source of inspiration and it is an honor to work with them every day. My heartfelt thanks to all of you. I hope our experiences and shared learnings benefit many others.

The team at Business Expert Press has been a delight to work with at every stage and identified that I had two books in one, hence the second book will be published next year.

I wish my mom, a voracious reader and lifelong learner could be here to see this. Among many gifts she shared, one of them was a lively curiosity. My dad inspired my passion for business and the outdoors. Karen, now, forever and always—love you.

My deep love, admiration and appreciation to Beth and Jake. I think you learned much about business and life around the dinner table; I know I did from you. I am proud of you and amazed at the adults you have become. I am a better person because of what I learn from you. PJ and Sam, I am grateful that you and your families have been such an integral part of our lives.

First, last and always, my love and gratitude goes to my husband Peter who has encouraged me, cajoled me, supported me, endorsed me and believed in me from the first day we met. You inspired my dreams and much of what we have achieved has been possible because of you.

# Introduction

I have the best job in the world. Every day I work with individuals, CEOs, and leadership teams of mid-sized companies and executives in Fortune 500 firms. Every leader I engage with wants to be successful and many of them reap the greatest satisfaction from seeing their companies and their employees succeed. Many of them are seasoned leaders and recognized long ago that their success is largely derived from the strength of their teams.

In my former life as a corporate executive, I was fortunate to have a few very good mentors. One of them taught me early on that most of my success would result from recruiting the best people. That was great advice. However, I learned that this action alone was insufficient to achieve my goals. Talented, passionate, committed, and motivated people will change the world—for their customers, their colleagues, their shareholders, and their employees. However, to unleash people's potential, to generate recurring revenue growth, foster innovation, and maximize productivity, we need to hold each other's feet to the fire. We need to create a culture of accountability.

Why has accountability emerged as a dominant theme? Consider the massive costs of our increasingly regulated environments. Like Sarbanes-Oxley (SOX), most regulation has been enacted in response to corporate and individual misconduct. The 2008 global financial crisis resulted largely from misdeeds fed by greed. Even after millions lost their jobs and their homes, regulation is still required to govern ethical behavior. In 2016, the US Labor Department announced regulations to ensure that financial advisors in the insurance and banking industries must act in their clients' best interests. When we regulate morality, taxpayers and companies of all sizes bear additional costs. As leaders, we may be able to mitigate the trend for ever-increasing regulation by creating more accountable organizations that foster ethical behavior and by rapidly stamping out misconduct in our firms.

What are the other benefits of an accountable organization? They are numerous. Increased employee engagement, higher ROI on projects, retention of your best performers, improved customer loyalty; greater innovation and increased profitability all result from higher levels of accountability. As the highest level of leadership performance is grounded in self-awareness, this book provides you with exercises, assessments, and stories to chart your leadership journey. You may choose to start at the beginning and read this systematically or pick and choose the sections that are most applicable to you at any given time. Whatever your approach, I wish you well on the journey. Leading others is an honor and a privilege. Continually seeking to understand how your own motivations, behaviors, and actions affect yourself and the people you interact with is a worthy lifelong pursuit.

# CHAPTER 1

# Creating a Culture of Accountability

Fostering accountability will be a game changer for you as a leader and for your organization. And it is simple. Maybe not easy but it is beautiful in its simplicity. The practices in this book have elevated the performance of companies and employees, across varied industries, corporate cultures, size, public or private, start-ups, and Fortune 100 companies.

Employee engagement is at an all-time low—a global epidemic, costing billions of dollars. One of the biggest contributors to this phenomenon is employees reporting a gap of accountability in their companies. When employee engagement increases, so do profits.

Organizations are often consumed with projects. These can include information technology projects ranging from $100,000s to $100,000,000s; post M&A integration; marketing projects when launching new products and services; capital projects such as power plants or new facilities; or office moves. In an accountable organization, projects generate higher return on investment. There are fewer mistakes, less rework, less onerous oversight, faster implementation, greater ownership, lower costs, higher customer satisfaction, and capital to deploy to other projects. Have I convinced you yet?

How does accountability foster innovation? With greater accountability, leaders and peers hold each other to account. Everyone knows they will be expected to meet their commitments and take responsibility for resolving issues. As a result, one can lessen time-consuming, costly, and demanding oversight. As you become more nimble, innovation increases. You may see more rapid research and development, streamlined planning cycles, and faster recovery from mistakes.

## Evaluating Your Workplace

What does a high level of accountability look like? Here are some of the most observable characteristics:

- Open and respectful conflict.
- Employees at all levels openly take responsibility for mistakes and make recommendations for change.
- Customer problem escalation is lower than your industry peers.
- The majority of projects are completed in accordance with the original schedule and budget *with the desired level of quality*.
- Few or declining health and safety incidents.
- Employees at all levels take holidays.
- Involuntary turnover of no less than three percent annually.
- Voluntary turnover of five to ten percent annually.

## When Accountability Is Lacking

There are a variety of reasons you may be experiencing a lack of accountability. It may be that most of the right behaviors exist and you simply need to make some fine-tuning.

Once you identify the contributors you are one step closer to closing the gaps. Here are some common factors that can undermine a culture of accountability.

- Executives have many competing priorities.
  - Managers expect people to meet their obligations and to follow through on commitments without prompting or probing questions. As a result, they may not follow up, even when their instincts and judgment are indicating otherwise. Over time, this can create an impression that leaders are not serious about their requirements and/or that resisting the company direction, not changing in response to feedback or resisting change will be rewarded.

- Unmet expectations.
  - Managers believe that their direct reports have a clear understanding of what is expected of them. Managers also often believe they know what their employees expect of them as leaders. This is not always the case. A lack of clarity can result in duplicated effort, wasted time, and missed opportunities. Investing time to confirm that expectations will reap benefits.
- Accountability conversations can be uncomfortable, so people avoid them.
  - Ironically, this discomfort often stems from leaders wondering, "Was I really clear in my expectations? Now I am going to tell him or her that they are not meeting my expectations. Is that fair?" Yes. It is fair and respectful—to the individual and, just as importantly, to their colleagues.
- Leaders do not know what they should do differently to create more accountability.
  - They are uncertain about what actions would demonstrate their own accountability and how to hold others to greater account without feeling like they are micromanaging.
- There is a misconception that holding people accountable takes more time.
  - It does not; it frees everyone to perform at a higher level.

Other contributors to a lack of accountability:

- When there are no visible repercussions for unmet commitments or marginal performance, a culture of lassitude results.
- A false belief that it is easier to accept the status quo than to address the anticipated resistance.
- Managers do not see the strong correlation between accountability and financial performance.
- Rationalization that remaining with the devil we know (e.g., supplier, business partner, or employee) is preferable and requires less effort than replacing them. That is only true for about ten minutes.

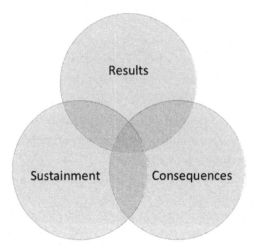

*Figure 1.1 The Building Blocks of Accountability*

Results, sustainment, and consequences are required to create an accountable company (Figure 1.1). If you have results and sustainment but lack consequences, you encounter a downward spiral. If you focus on results with consequences but do not sustain the practices, you will engender employee disengagement and customer dissatisfaction. If you have sustainment and consequences without a focus on results, you will have busy work. Having any two of the building blocks without the third creates opportunity costs for the company.

## *Results*

Being "busy" has become a badge of honor in Western society. Frenetic actions, long to-do lists, achievement-oriented updates on social media have become the norm. Within organizations, a similar approach can contribute to a misplaced focus. Accountable and high-performing leaders pay attention to results over activities.

## *Sustainment*

When companies follow through on commitments and operate in a consistent manner, it creates integrity with customers and employees. When you operate in a sustained manner, you avoid the trap of situational behavior. Situational leadership can occur in good and bad times, although it occurs most times when there are problems in the company. As an example, when a competitor is gaining market share, creating risk to profitability, reputation and customer retention, executives are likely to take a more proactive stance with the sales team and perhaps the marketing and product groups. Typically the leaders will follow up more often, will review performance metrics more frequently, and they may recognize actions taken by employees to address the problem.

When life returns to normal again, when sales return and the company regains market share, most executives and middle management will turn their attention elsewhere. That is appropriate as the immediate issue has been resolved. However, accountable behavior should continue. This includes clearly setting objectives, measuring and documenting performance results, following through on commitments, and addressing gaps in performance. This is sustained management of accountability.

### *Consequences*

Within a culture of accountability, when results do not meet expectations, there are consequences. Remember, success is achieved through measuring results, not activities. If the technology projects within a company are often behind schedule and over budget, an accountable president will ask the chief information officer (CIO) to document what actions she is taking to address the issues and what results will be achieved by what date. If the results do not show improvement over time and if the president has assisted the CIO by removing any obstacles, eventually the CIO will have to change roles or leave the organization. Accountable leaders do not allow substandard performance to be tolerated even if it is a long-service employee, well-liked individual, or someone who has deep technical knowledge. If the performance is not a behavior issue (e.g., disrespect or harassment), the employee may be able to remain with the company in a role to which they are better suited. This rarely works well, in the long run; however, so I do not recommend it.

## Establishing Accountability in Your Culture

1. *Define success.* Leaders and employees cannot strive for the desired results if the end state is not clearly defined. This is not about interim goals. It is the company or division's vision and mission or the team's raison d'etre.
2. *Create and communicate the greater purpose.* Seventy percent of U.S. workers are disengaged. Work without a greater purpose is dissatisfying. Aspiring to something that matters motivates most of us. How does what an individual is doing contribute in a bigger way? Identify how performing their daily activities, with excellence, contribute to something bigger. Explain why and how what they do matters (e.g., how does their performance contribute to share price; to healthy clients; to their coworkers and contractors all returning safely home to their families; to others achieving their retirement dreams).
3. *Set clear goals: specific and measurable.* Review progress against results on a regular basis, ideally once per month (once per quarter for more senior staff).
4. *Recognize and celebrate people who take responsibility for mistakes.* Own up to your own errors. Share what you learned and what you will do differently next time. Expect the same from others.
5. *Take action on poor performance.* Discuss missed performance expectations. Document repeated performance gaps. Tie compensation to performance.
6. *Do not tolerate behavior that is not aligned to corporate values.* Discuss the behavior as soon as possible after it occurs. Call it out, respectfully, in a group setting, if appropriate. Here is an example. "Dan, I understand you are frustrated. However, this is not the way we speak to each other at this company."

Fostering accountability requires self-awareness and personal accountability, leadership of others, and effectively running your business or area of responsibility. Chapters 2–4 provide self-assessments and guide you through your own career choices and personal effectiveness. Chapters 5–9 provide tools and resources to elevate your leadership of others.

# CHAPTER 2

# Establishing a Career without Sacrificing a Life

Over the span of two generations, family and work lives have changed dramatically. Dual career couples are the norm. Women fought for equal compensation than their male counterparts and also for the opportunity to be considered for the same roles as men—from firefighters to law enforcement, military to senior executives of Fortune 500 enterprises. While the progress in North America has been slower than many expected, the landscape reflects greater diversity in traditionally male occupations and a larger number of women in director and vice president roles in corporations.

The next frontier is equality for men . . . enabling them to make choices that benefit their families and fulfill their personal interests. In 2000, federal policy in Canada extended parental leaves to twelve months. The leave can be shared between both the parents. Several years later, most male professionals are reluctant to take advantage of this benefit, as taking a leave is not widely accepted as demonstrating commitment to one's career.

There is an interesting emerging trend of young professionals pursuing unconventional work such as serial contracts or using the Internet to much more broadly market and source their freelance offerings in areas like web design, ghostwriting, travel blogs, and so on. This book is intended for professionals working in corporate environments—mid- and large-sized firms, government, and not-for-profits—so we will explore successful strategies for these environments.

An excellent role model for this is Cathy Backman. With over thirty years in corporate roles, many of them at the executive level, Cathy is highly respected for leading transformational change in complex and varied businesses. When I met her several years ago, she was a senior vice president for a large firm. She joked that she had created and piloted a wide variety of alternate work options. These included job sharing, part time, and leaves of absence.

This was an anomaly at the time and unfortunately in many situations, continues to be. Why is this? In some cases, executives are not demonstrably supportive of alternative work options, even when they have been endorsed by the organization. In many cases, however, leaders are apprehensive to request an alternate work option for fear that they will be seen as uncommitted to their career progression. Cathy is an example of someone who overcame this fear and charted a path that worked well for her and her company. How did she accomplish this?

> "It's important to check in with yourself on a regular basis to determine the relative importance of family, career, community, friends, and investment in self. I found the relative importance of each can and does change through life. It's important to be honest with this assessment and then fine-tune your life plan to align with your priorities.
>
> While family has always been my top priority, I found the relative importance of the remaining four categories changed over time and I adjusted my plan accordingly. After being extremely career driven, I was surprised how strongly I felt about the need to spend more time with the girls when they were young. This was in the early 1990s well before flexible work arrangements existed at TD, or for that matter at many companies. After much reflection, I came to the decision that I would do my best to find a reduced work schedule to accommodate my increased family demands and resolved that if I didn't find something I would resign and look for an employer who would meet my new flexible work needs. Fortunately, I went on to do three or four progressively senior roles with TD over a seven-year period, all of which were variations of flexible work arrangements including a condensed work week, three days/week, four days a week, and working from home. All were done on a "pilot" basis, as TD didn't have any defined policies at the time. Ultimately, it was a "win–win" for the company and me. Their flexibility and willingness to engage in a few pilots kept me in the game and made me extremely loyal

> to the company. In my last seven years with the bank I championed a brand new bank wide Flexible Work Arrangement Committee as their Chair and set in motion the creation of a number of Flexible Work Arrangement Policies. With appointed senior throughout the company, we made substantial progress.
>
> Although we made substantial progress in removing the stigma associated with career-oriented woman wanting to work flexible work arrangements, it was still relatively frowned upon if senior women (VP and up) wanted to partake in the arrangements. Regardless, I viewed is as substantive progress up to the AVP level."
>
> —Cathy Backman, former division vice president, ADP and former senior vice president, strategy and solutions, TD Bank

While our careers play a dominant role in our lives, when advising others I often suggest them consider the phrase "To everything there is a season . . ." (Ecclesiastes 3:1). Do not set yourself up for disappointment or frustration by creating a single prototype of career success. There are a variety of approaches and by remaining open to alternatives you may achieve greater career progression and satisfaction than you had originally planned. It is also important to remain flexible. You may utilize different approaches at certain stages of your career in response to varying personal demands.

## Models that Work

### Full Time

Although you may consider full-time work to be the preferred or default option, there are interesting variations that are worth pursuing.

### Alternate Full Time and/or Demanding Roles with Your Spouse

I have seen several couples successfully navigate the demands of family and work commitments by alternating when they occupied demanding roles and/or when each of them worked full time. Flexibility, mutual respect, and compromise were the common characteristics in these situations.

Cathy Riggall and Keith Potte have been married for over forty years, raised two sons and managed to balance two careers with family and community life. Now retired, they look back on what made it all work. Cathy summed it up in the phrase: "we did not have it all, but we had what we wanted."

Both managed to achieve success in in their jobs, by deciding early that the most important thing in a job was that it had to be interesting. For Keith this meant moving from highway engineering to marketing and to a number of CEO positions in food production companies. Cathy spent most of her career in the financial services industry, holding senior positions in two of Canada's large banks and trust companies. Her career finished with a ten-year stint as ice president, business affairs at the University of Toronto. She claims that her career path, more accurately described as a meander, left her uniquely qualified to take on the role at U of T, which was rather like running a small city. "Changing jobs was not always a matter of choice, but we did try not to get fired at the same time."

Along the way, Cathy was involved in a variety of volunteer positions from scorekeeping and statistician for her sons' baseball league to president of YWCA Toronto. Keith declined to get involved in any volunteer position that required him to attend meetings, but was happy to be the team manager for his son's hockey team and was the chauffeur to all of their various activities.

"We agreed soon after our first son was born that the kids would be a priority and that we would be there to support them, no matter what they wanted to do, even if we had no interest at all in whatever it was. Our son still laughs at the memory of Keith sitting in the stands with head phones on, listening to music and reading a book" said Cathy.

Ultimately they claim that what made achieving life–work balance was having a range of interests outside of work. Reading, theater, hiking, travel, and family all kept them from falling into the trap of all work and nothing else. Now that their kids have kids, and they are retired, they still spend time doing the things they like to do. They just have more time for them.

As recently as a decade ago, job candidates were considered most attractive if they were actively employed. Fortunately, the cycles of downsizing commencing in the 1980s have changed that perception. Recruiters and hiring executives recognize that talented professionals may not be employed on a continuous basis, whether by choice or circumstance.

Work–life balance is best measured over a month and a year, not a day or a week. Too many of us have experienced grief chasing an unattainable measure of work–life balance. Although balance can be achieved, it must be measured over several months or a year, not over the course of a week or your typical workday. Executive roles require commitment, flexibility, often travel, and may demand your participation in external pursuits such as boards, community events, and so on. If you aspire to a senior role, you need to realistically assess where you will invest your time and your energy. The ubiquitous nature of technology feels like we are required to be always on. However, you have tremendous control over how you utilize technology and respond to the demands placed upon you.

Although some management and most executive roles may not yet lend themselves to part time, they do, however, provide greater flexibility. Because you are not punching a clock, you will typically be measured more for your results than the hours of face time in the office. This can enable you to attend your children's events during the day or accompany an aging parent to a medical appointment. Alternatively, it may facilitate your ability to participate in community activities such as sitting on a board. Typically you are able to plan further in advance for holiday absences so you can allocate time for important events. In leadership roles, you can often delegate responsibility to one or more of your subordinates, providing them with growth and development. In senior roles, you may also be able to engage in a sabbatical to pursue an MBA or a volunteer commitment.

## *Part Time*

Part-time work is no longer relegated to retail jobs or call center roles. Many professional jobs can be conducted on a part-time basis. You may also pull back from the demands of a full-time role while pursuing an executive MBA or other demanding professional development. Your offer to reduce hours may be particularly well received during an economic downturn or period of belt buckling. It is surprising how many people do not make these requests for fear that their boss will not react favorably.

### Compressed Workweek

For a period of time when my children were young, I worked a compressed workweek. I completed my 37.5 hours in four days rather than five. We all benefited from my having one day a week to run errands, play with the kids or complete household chores, freeing me up for more fun time on the weekends.

### Telecommuting

The ubiquitous nature of technology has enabled remote work and telecommuting more than ever before. Engineering, sales, medical research, journalism, marketing, supply chain services, graphic design, human resource functions, and many others can be fulfilled from home offices or satellite locations.

Senior professional jobs can be highly conducive to working remotely. At large banks, district vice presidents have responsibility for retail bank branches spread across a geographic area. While they regularly attend meetings in corporate offices, many of them conduct most of their work in their branch locations or via technology from their home offices. Professors also conduct their work in a variety of locations—on campus for meetings and some teaching, from a variety of locations for supporting virtual students or conducting research. IBM has been very progressive in enabling remote. A 2010 Information Week article cited IBM as having two hundred thousand home office workers.[1]

### Satellite Offices

In large cities such as Houston, New York, and London, many office dwellers commute from densely populated suburban canters. Some

---

[1] *http://www.informationweek.com/it-leadership/radical-ibm-200000-home-office-workers/d/d-id/1089553?*

progressive organizations have studied the commuting patterns of their employees and discovered that many of their employees live in a small number of popular bedroom communities. By opening satellite offices in these suburban locations, everyone benefits.

Without a lengthy commute, people have more energy for their work and their families. Often the satellite locations can offer fitness facilities or a child care center that are cost prohibitive in the urban centers. As a result, reported employee engagement and productivity improve. In most cases, employee turnover declines. When you consider the average cost of replacing someone is 1 to 1.5 times their total annual compensation, these savings are considerable. These companies are able to attract new qualified professionals who live and want to work in the suburbs. In addition to the productivity gains and reduced expenses of turnover, companies reduce facilities costs, as leaseholds are typically less in the outlying communities than for urban towers. As far back as 2007, a Bloomberg article cited IBM as saving $100 million annually.[2]

### Building Your Case for an Alternative Work Option

As a corporate executive, I was always most amenable to and gave greatest consideration to a well-thought-out business case. If you are considering an alternate work option—remote work, reduced work hours or part-time work, a sabbatical or other—first conduct your research and prepare well for your conversation with your boss. Be prepared for the fact while it may not be approved for your current position, your manager may suggest an alternate role. If that would be a nonstarter for you, know that in advance.

Also ensure the timing is right. Have you:

- Spent three or more years with the company?
- Been in your current role for more than one year *or* are you applying to a new role in the company and that role bodes well for an alternative work option?

---

[2] *http://www.bloomberg.com/bw/stories/2007-02-12/working-from-home-its-in-the-detailsbusinessweek-business-news-stock-market-and-financial-advice*

- Received a recent performance rating indicating your performance was meeting or exceeding expectations?
- Fostered a good relationship with your immediate manager and, ideally, their manager, if appropriate (i.e., if you are not reporting directly to the CEO). If you report to the CEO, prepare him or her well for any required discussion with the board.
- Ensured you are financially and physically healthy, as a reduction in hours may result in less income and/or a reduction in benefits coverage?
- Researched and understood any impact on your pension or years of service calculations?

*Present Situation*

Although this business case should be in a narrative, I have used bullets to identify points for consideration as you craft your plan. Keep your business case to one page. If it is any longer, it will lose its effectiveness.

Items to keep in mind when building your plan:

- Length of time with organization
- Tenure in current role
- Cite achievements of the past twelve to eighteen months
- Other relevant information (e.g., completing a masters program, providing caregiving to friend or family member, change in health status for you or someone close to you).
- Your interest in an alternative work option
- Duration—are you asking for a permanent reduction in hours, for a specific length of time to complete further education, and so on?

*Options*

It is ideal if you can propose more than one option. This allows your leader a series of choices rather than simply a yes or no. This increases your likelihood that you can find a workable solution together.

Your options may include:

- Working from home one day per week or twice per month
- Working from a satellite office or field location on a prescribed schedule
- Compressed workweek (e.g., four days every week or four days for three weeks of every four).
- Reduced hours/part time
- Another identified, vacant role in the company for which part-time hours would be particularly appropriate

What are the benefits to the company?

- Provide accurate financial estimates—savings in salary and benefits expenses.
- Does this contribute to the development of others and therefore succession planning for the firm? If you are proposing a leave of absence, who have you identified that could fill in during your absence? If you are in a senior or leadership role, ideally you have two or more candidates. Do they have the skills and experience to step in easily or is it a development opportunity? How will you support them to ensure that they are successful?
- Are there reduced facilities costs if you are foregoing an office to work from home or are offering to share an office with another part-time employee?
- Will your productivity increase, as you will have a reduced commute?

### *Request for Approval*

- Identify preferred option or order of preference of multiple options.
- Start date—provide as much lead-time as possible.
- Commitment—confirm your commitment to meet or exceed all expectations of your role

- Offer a pilot? Like investing in a test market initiative, your leader may be more comfortable in approving a three-month pilot.
- Identify key performance indicators (KPIs) and commit to reviewing them at the end of a pilot or after eight weeks. These could include attending all important, predetermined meetings or conference calls, continued strong performance from your direct reports, department or division, sustained or improved performance on key deliverables.
- Out clause—indicate that you understand the organization has the right to terminate the arrangement and ask that you do as well and cite a notice period of one month or other.

## Encouraging and Accommodating Work Models

Consider how these different working models can be incorporated into your teams. Knowledge professionals are seeking viable options and realistic working practices that enable them to sustain strong families, contribute to their communities, and maintain meaningful careers. With insufficient work options in most corporations, minimal parental leaves in the United States, and little visible support for men taking personal or child care leaves, proactively offering alternative work models will contribute to employee engagement, heightened productivity and retention. The benefit of this is increased profitability through attraction and retention of high-quality, talented people. Many employees will struggle indefinitely before seeking alternative working models. This is costly to the company. Consider selectively offering options to your best employees.

## Developing Leadership Athleticism
## © 2015 Lorraine Moore

Many of us are drawn to executive roles for the variety afforded by the intellectual and mental challenge, the ability to make a meaningful contribution, the prestige and the influence we can wield. These are demanding roles typically requiring long days, attendance at community events, socializing and, in many cases, frequent travel. In the same way that athletes best perform when they sustain consistent healthy habits, so it is with high-performing leaders.

Leadership athleticism has the following hallmarks: resilience, speed, flexibility, and mental acuity.

### Resilience

Resilience is the ability to sustain energy, mental attention, tolerance, and optimal health for extended periods of time, particularly during exceptional times such as a hostile takeover, numerous employee layoffs, severe economic constraints such as the 2008 global financial crisis and plummeting oil prices commencing in 2015, or a brand damaging and ethical crisis such as a large-scale safety incident.

> In 2008, a suspected 22 Canadians died from exposure to listeria bacteria on McCain packaged meats. Michael McCain, CEO, demonstrated considerable resilience and leadership in the days and weeks following the incident. With a haggard appearance, he rapidly made public statements taking full responsibility for the incident and apologized to families and customers. He gained tremendous respect from consumers who valued and trusted his transparency and his presence during a stressful time.

### Speed

Leaders may be called upon to meet increased demands with little or no warning. This requires the ability to make important decisions rapidly and sometimes without all the facts.

### Flexibility

You must be able to change course quickly, without lamenting for long the lost career-making deal, the failed acquisition, or the disappointing product launch before identifying your new course of action.

### Mental Acuity

Most professional jobs and certainly all leadership and executive roles require complex mental functioning. Mental acuity is required to most effectively process the considerable volume of information and data at your disposal and the varying opinions provided internally and externally. This is not only a measure of intelligence, but also your ability to concentrate, focus, and understand. Mental acuity is heightened with sufficient sleep, physical exercise, mental breaks, and creative pursuits.

***Methods to Develop Leadership Athleticism***

- No pretend time off (PTO)
- Physical health
- Live the examined life
- Energy management
- Keep it fresh

Let us explore each of these.

1. No PTO allowed.
   - Take your holidays.
     - No matter how ego building it may seem to boast your accumulation of untaken holidays, you are setting a poor example to others and implying that to be successful, they must follow your lead.
     - Without real holidays, you neglect your physical health. You may think you operate best on continued adrenaline highs. Our bodies are not built that way. Sustained high levels of cortisol drain your adrenals and set you up for disturbed sleep and more frequent viruses.
     - You are also neglecting your mental health. Creativity diminishes when you do not give your mind a break. Creativity soars when you expose your mind to art, music, and laughter. Your creativity enables you to conceive fresh ideas and new approaches to business problems.
     - If you must remain connected to the office while on holiday, discipline yourself and others. Spend thirty to forty-five minutes each day to read and respond to urgent issues only.

- Use this time off for activities and locations that feed your body and spirit—exercise, naps, mediation, prayer, sports, music, arts, culture, entertaining, a walk on the beach, a day in the mountains, and so on.
- Take at least one full-day off each weekend. Two days are even better. Many of my senior clients feel a responsibility to be available. While laudable, this is not an excuse to read and send e-mails throughout every evening and weekend. If your company has a major issue such as a cyber-security breach, a major customer or employee issue, someone will pick up the phone and call you!

2. Physical health—hold your own two feet to the fire.
   - Pay as much attention to your health and wellness as you do your professional success. Your body will better cope with the long workdays, changing time zones, and mental stress of an executive job when you are fit. This may be surprising but the biggest contributor to brain health, memory, attention, and mental acuity is physical exercise. The benefits of mind games such as Sudoku and Luminosity are secondary to a cardiovascular workout.
   - If you are overweight, smoke, or have high blood pressure, take charge of your health. We know that the biggest killers, heart attacks and strokes, are largely lifestyle induced. Researchers now attribute as many as seventy percent of cancers to lifestyle causes as well.
   - Ideally, exercise five times per week for a minimum of twenty minutes. Building muscle mass and bone density is crucially important for long-term health so incorporate strength training to represent as much as fifty percent of your working out time.

3. Live the examined life—from reflection and meditation flow creativity.
   - Our busyness, feeling important, and being needed feed our ego but it does not feed our souls. Even ten minutes of meditation benefit your mental acuity and physical health. Sometimes we stay busy to avoid underlying feels of discontent.
   - Create time for reflection. You can achieve this by:
     - Turning off your music or radio on your commute. Allow your mind to wander.
     - Taking a walk in the evening with no ear buds.

- Closing the door of your office for ten minutes. Turn off your cell phone and forward your calls.
- I have even found I can reflect in an airport lounge if I put in my ear buds, no music and find a corner away from the fray.
- Finding opportunities for reflection in a yoga class, a run, fishing, laying on the grass with your kids, and identifying animal shapes in the clouds.
- In my experience, executives who make time for reflection are much better leaders. They achieve insights during quieter moments. These insights inform higher quality decisions. Reflection provides clarity and a calm that extends to their relationships with others.

---

I have a longtime friend who is a well-respected professional. His family often took holidays in Europe. He recounted a Sunday evening in Portugal. It is about 10:30 p.m. They were outside enjoying the sights and sounds. His children were running around with cousins, he was enjoying a glass of port on the lawn with family and friends. All of the others had demanding professional jobs like he did but they were not on holiday. He turned to one of them and asked,

"Is this a typical Sunday night?"
"Yes," replied his cousin. "Why, what would you be doing at home?"
"I would be lying in bed worrying about the upcoming work week" he replied.

Reflecting on this discussion later he realized that part of his overwork was an effort to avoid thinking about the fact that his life was out of balance. He knew this but pushed the thoughts aside as he could not conceive a way out of the trap of his commitments. With further reflection and discussion with his wife, he left the demanding law practice and became an in-house counsel for a large organization. He is much happier.

*Exercise 1: Reflective Question*

You may find it useful to have a prepared list of questions to guide your reflective time. Some people find this providing a more satisfying experience. Topics can include relationships, work, travel, financial, physical health, spirituality, and so on.

- Where am I achieving the greatest satisfaction in my work?
- Where would I like to improve relationships with friends or family?
- Where would I like to travel?
- What hobbies did I really enjoy when I was young?
- Do I have unmet passions or interests? For example, learning a new language, taking up sailing, attending a cooking class, and so on.
- What is one thing I could change that would improve the quality of my life?

1. Energy management—not time management or work–life balance.
    - It was a very fortunate day for me when a mentor advised me to prioritize energy rather than time management. Life most high achievers, I thrive when faced with complex business challenges, variety, demands and diversity. Even travel energizes me—not the process of travel but varied surroundings, culture, food, language, business, and personal cultures. I had no trouble attacking and completing all tasks on a lengthy and daunting to-do list. My challenge *was* that those around me typically did not understand nor share my drive or my capacity and did not have the same low boredom threshold that I did.
    - Of course, like everyone, my energy is not boundless and if I did not manage my energy, I became more susceptible to cold viruses and/or felt overwhelmed and fatigued.
2. Keep it fresh.
    - Take the initiative to seek out new opportunities at least every three years. You need not leave your firm but speak openly with your leadership about what next role will best round out

your development, maximize your strengths, and benefit the organization.
- Attend association meetings for your industry. Become more actively involved by joining the board or assisting at an industry event.
- Network and/or formally meet with executives in other industries. Many CEOs participate in forum groups with peers from other industries.
- Attend executive development programs through a renowned college. Stanford, Harvard, Queens, and others offer a variety of programs.
- Hold a formal career-planning discussion with each of your direct reports every year. Hold them accountable for preparing for the meeting. Ask and expect them to come to the meeting with a list of ideas and options. If they do not prepare, reschedule the meeting and confirm that they have a responsibility to be prepared.

> TD Bank has an effective and active talent management and succession-planning program. Executives and leaders at all levels are held accountable to identify individuals with potential for more senior roles and/or lateral moves. Formal reviews are conducted every year. Each leader's performance is measured, in part, by how well she or he develops their employees. One of the benefits of this is that high-performing employees move throughout the organization, establishing a broader network of colleagues and acquiring greater understanding of and, ideally, empathy for other areas of the company. With this knowledge, they are better positioned to identify and remove gaps—exploiting synergies and benefiting shareholders, customers, and employees.
>
> Contrast this with organizations that primarily promote leaders within a functional area such as operations, IS marketing, research and development, and so on. In some companies, this stems from the high value that they place on functional knowledge. The downside is the missed opportunities exploited by an organization like TD.

For you as a leader, a one trick pony is not as valuable or marketable as someone with a greater breadth of experience. It is much easier for boredom and complacency to set in. Both of these are killers of leadership athleticism, not to mention professional and personal satisfaction.

## Healthy Support Networks

No man or woman is an island. Supportive relationships are correlated with greater health, longevity, successful careers, and high-functioning relations with family and friends. Support networks can arise from a variety of places. The common factors are:

- Reciprocal relationship with an exchange of ideas, learning, sharing, and time allotted for each of you to seek advice, offer feedback, and so on.
- Candid communication that is caring and also honest; people who can tell you what you need to hear.
- Mutual respect.
- Common interests or knowledge.

These can be personal or professional relationships. A mix of both is best. As referenced earlier in this chapter, many CEOs utilize peer forums in this manner. I consistently and actively participate in and contribute to a global community of experts, acting as an accountability partner on occasion, offering encouragement, sharing ideas, providing feedback, and offering advice. Many professionals participate in industry associations for the same reasons.

Weight Watchers and Alcoholics Anonymous are other examples of long-standing, formalized affiliations that have thrived due to accountability, education, support, and affiliation.

Ideally, personal relationships are nurturing and round us out. Spouses and close friends may place less value on our corporate success. This has multiple benefits, including keeping our egos in check. For examples, our intrinsic value is not tied to our stock price and our "authority" may carry little weight outside of the office, they remind us of the fun elements of life—hobbies, leisure, recreation, and wonder and they will bolster our spirits and cheer us on, regardless of circumstance. As highly successful professionals, few of us are comfortable expressing vulnerability. This is unfortunate; as doing so actually makes us more appealing and respected by others. Friendships can provide an opportunity to share our fears and anxieties.

Remember, the key is a healthy support network. Stop spending time with people who leave you feeling disenchanted or discouraged or individuals who actively compete with you. Release guilt or feelings of obligation. To be your best and achieve your best, you must be selective in deciding who you will spend time with. Elite athletes hire the best coaches and train with those who outperform them. Take a lesson from their playbook.

In summary, evaluate the quality of your support network. Do you have a strong network and simply need to prioritize time with individuals and/or a group? Or is it time for you seek out and/or deepen relationships with others? A diverse composition can be highly beneficial—a mix of personal and professional, with colleagues from different industries, countries, roles, and so on.

A healthy support network can be comprised of:

- Spouse
- Friends
- Business acquaintances, colleagues, or peers
- Board chair or director
- Industry association member

## Moore's Map to Success©

Stephen Covey's enduring statement "begin with the end in mind," has far-reaching applicability. It is a useful premise for developing a strategic plan, launching a new product, evaluating your financial plan, and creating or updating your personal roadmap.

I like to start with a day in the distant future. This stokes your creative juices rather than considering simple course adjustments. The key is to think big!!! Regrets rarely result from not achieving momentous goals. Regrets arise from playing small, holding back for fear of failure and from playing it safe. As in figure 2.1, life will offer interesting opportunities and also sometimes, unexpected detours. Be flexible to respond to the positive unexpected detours and opportunities.

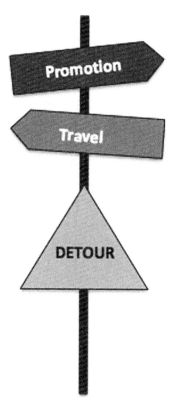

*Figure 2.1 Charting Your Course*

*Exercise 2: Building Your Roadmap*

Step 1   Pick a date at least ten years in the future or as far in the future as you would like it to be. Some clients have used retirement from their current career; others have picked their ninetieth birthday.

Step 2   Consider who you most admire and why. If possible, identify three people. What characteristics do these individuals embody that you most highly value?

Step 3   For each of the following categories, define one to three ideal outcomes and/or achievements. Consider your legacy and your contribution in each of these areas. How would you like to be known by those who matter? What would you like to be recognized for?

| Career | Relationships |
|---|---|
| • .... <br> • .... <br> • .... | • .... <br> • .... <br> • .... |
| Health and Wellness <br> • .... <br> • .... <br> • .... | Travel, Leisure, and Recreation <br> • .... <br> • .... <br> • .... |

## Example

| Career | Relationships |
|---|---|
| • Contributed to ABC Company achieving unprecedented success for shareholders, employees, and customers <br> • Company ABC recognized as industry leader in innovation <br> • Provided challenging, meaningful, and rewarding work for thousands of people through my leadership | • A loving and supportive relationship with my partner <br> • Highly respectful, loving, adventurous laughter-filled relationships with my spouse and children <br> • Took each of the children for a long weekend trip on their own for their sixteenth birthday |
| Health and wellness <br> • Consistently participated in exercise program utilizing personal trainer <br> • Completed annual physical check-ups <br> • Rediscovered my love of rowing/hockey/ swimming | Travel, Leisure, and Recreation <br> • .... <br> • .... <br> • .... |

Step 4   Considering your goals in the above categories, create your legacy statement for that future date—in a few sentences.

## Example

*In spring 20XX, I will celebrate my good health and satisfying career success with name and name and name. I will be grateful for my rewarding relationships with name or friend, partner, son, or daughter. My work with the X foundation has been very enriching and I am glad I could share my talents with the community.*

Step 5   As you gaze to the future, what is the one adjustment you could make that would have a material and positive impact on you achieving your legacy and some of the goals above?

# CHAPTER 3

# Constructing Your Leadership Brand

In this chapter, we will explore why it is important to proactively create and/or maintain your reputation and image. We will review what it means to have a personal brand and why this will be a lasting requirement and not a passing fad.

Consider the value of corporate brands. Accounting practices recognize the value of a company brand and capture this as goodwill on balance sheets. Goodwill denotes the value of the company's brand and image in the marketplace, a valuation beyond the tangible assets of inventory, people, buildings, cash, and investments.

> Tata Motors acquired Jaguar and Range Rover from Ford for $2.56 billion. The value of this transaction extended well beyond the value of all tangible assets and reflected the prestige associated with the Jaguar and Range Rover names and image. Similarly, Kraft paid $19.5 billion for Cadbury. It would not have been difficult for Kraft to duplicate the products and Cadbury did not have any unique manufacturing capabilities. The value was in the name, a long-standing staple of high-quality chocolate, particularly in Europe. So it is with your brand. The value of your brand, the strength of your reputation is derived from much more than your title, education, and credentials.

Many years ago a wise mentor taught me that people's agendas and motivations are much more visible than they realize. That was a great lesson for me. I started to more actively observe others while also giving greater scrutiny to my own actions and underlying drivers. We each portray an image whether intentional or not and whether conscious or not. This image and our personal brand is a by-product of our speech, dress, body language, our affiliations, and actions.

We will explore each of these factors. What image do you portray and what image do you wish to portray?

In the area of leadership, there is a set of attributes that contribute favorably on one's brand. These include courageous leadership, executive presence, visibility, brevity of communication, and judgment.

Let us address a few of these characteristics.

## Courageous Leadership

The term courageous leadership has been utilized by a variety of leaders. For me it embodies the following characteristics:

- Willing to identify issues or problems, particularly when the subject is sensitive or the opinion may be unpopular.
- Regularly encourage others to challenge your beliefs, biases or views on the company, a sanctioned project, product or service.
- Address poor performance, with compassion and respect. Do not avoid the situation hoping it will improve.
- Hold yourself accountable. Hold others accountable.
- Admit when you are wrong or when you made a mistake.
- Move forward. Make a decision even when: you may not have fully analyzed all the data; not everyone agrees; you are less than one hundred percent ready; it may fail but if successful it will be better for the organization and/or its customers employees, shareholders.

> John Coates is a senior research fellow in neuroscience at the University of Cambridge. His research identified that when we are under stress, our propensity for risk-taking decreases. This is highly relevant for leaders as risk-taking behavior is considered a useful leadership attribute and will contribute positively to your image, your perceived performance, and your likelihood of promotion.

One of the wisest decisions you can take is to accept leadership for a troubled or underperforming project, team, department, or division. Often, people shy away from these situations; that is a mistake. In accepting the challenging responsibility, in the worst-case you will make minimal but with noticeable improvements. As a result, others will recognize the forward progress and will applaud you for improving a poor situation. In the best-case scenario, you will dramatically improve the situation—increasing revenue, reducing risk, addressing customer dissatisfaction, improving safety performance, or enhancing employee morale. You are likely to receive a great deal of recognition for your ability to generate value for the organization and to resolve challenging situations. This can have a significant and long-standing positive impact to your brand, heightening your perceived value to the organization and your potential for more responsibility.

> "Debbie" was offered a role as operations manager, client processing for a large insurance company. She was uncertain if she should accept the role. The employee engagement scores were the lowest in the history of the company and turnover was a concern. Client satisfaction scores were in the single digits compared to a corporate average of eighty-six percent. There was a large backlog of work, recurring financial losses and errors in processing. In addition to all this, pending regulatory changes would require a significant investment in technology to remain compliant. The executive leadership team was reluctant to invest multimillions in a business line that was losing money and damaging the corporate brand. After consulting with one of her mentors and me, Debbie accepted the role.
>
> In the first several months, disgruntled employees flowed through Debbie's office as if through a revolving door. The corporate lawyers regularly sought updates on how quickly her team would achieve compliance and her largest customers sometimes yelled in frustration and threatened to take their business to a competitor.

Debbie demonstrated many aspects of courageous leadership. She flew to client sites, met with their senior management, apologized and took accountability for the situation. She stood in front of her employees at a town hall meeting and asked for their commitment to remain with the department while she and her management team addressed the problems. After careful consideration she restructured the leadership team by terminating the poor performers. She did not shy away from delivering bad news when required (e.g., a new financial loss or client errors).

Within two years, customer satisfaction soared by sixty-five percent. Staff turnover was a problem of the past and a large technology project to ensure compliance, was well underway. It would be some time before the organization completely restored their reputation but they had not lost any clients in several months. Debbie and her staff celebrated their many successes. The executive leadership identified Debbie as having potential to take on more senior roles in the organization. They recognized her as someone who would provide calm leadership in difficult situations, who would step up to tough challenges and would take personal accountability thus demonstrating integrity to customers and employees.

You may find it interesting to complete the Courageous Leadership assessment© at the end of this chapter.

## Executive Presence

"At the end of every week, I can look back and say I have learned something new."

Walter is the vice president of Pipeline Integrity for Enbridge. He regularly liaises with community groups, landowners, aboriginal groups, provincial and federal politicians, the board, his colleagues, and staff. Among this diverse stakeholder group, he has the reputation as someone who embodies executive presence.

I asked him how he has achieved this.

"I think it has to do with being able to explain [the goals and expectations] in a universal language that creates alignment at every level. I have to be able to rally everyone and create alignment from the front line worker to my peers to the board. I am responsible for linking everyone together. I create a consistent message and hone that message."

If you complicate your life by trying to make your alignment approach different for different audiences, it is ineffective.

"Not everyone wants to know what is behind [a decision or the plan]. They want the confidence that I know what is behind it all."

Creating executive presence results from "a way of speaking [and a consistent message that] results in great understanding at all levels."

At an executive level, "you are lucky to have a level of authority. Begin by putting life in perspective. At this level, you have the power to crusade. You have the resources and authority to crusade. You may be viewed as a black sheep; but don't let that stop you. Utilize interpersonal relationships. Understand that influencing change within our organizations is a political process. People will get on the train."

It is likely that with little deliberation you can identify someone who exhibits executive presence. Your ability to do so may result from exposure to poised, articulate and authentic executives or because you have observed so little of what you would consider executive presence in your industry or organization. Executive presence is tangible, comprised of a set of skills that may not be innate and can be learned.

For ease of identification, the characteristics can be grouped into three categories:

***Physical presence:*** people described as having executive presence are typically described as: displaying poise, calm, attentive, with good listening skills, an unhurried and confident manner.

***Style:*** their behavior is consistent. Their staff and others can anticipate their reactions; therefore, they can be relied upon to respond consistently to challenging situations as well as the day-to-day situation. They demonstrate strategic thinking and operate with a widely communicated vision for the future. They are equally comfortable in social situations and put others at ease.

> The following is a humorous story that illustrates the skill of putting others at ease. My late father-in-law, Jake Moore, held a number of executive positions around the world. A courageous leader and a veteran General from World War II, he held uncompromising standards and a high degree of ethics. Occupying a reputation for being tough, sometimes ruthless, in his leadership of global companies, his opponents treaded carefully.
>
> While he spent much of his time working in the UK and Brazil, he relished time in his Canadian homes. One day my husband opened the door of his parents' home to a new guest who said she had a "lovely visit with the gardener for the past 30 minutes." The gentleman tending the flowers, spade in hand, dressed in hat, rumpled shorts and a t-shirt was in fact, the often feared corporate leader, Jake Moore.

*Character:* while perhaps not immediately visible, a leader with executive presence embodies integrity, solid judgment and is ethical in his or her practices. Decisions are made based on what is best for the organization before what is best for oneself. Leaders with high character make decisions grounded in solid judgment and they hold themselves and others to a high standard.

You may find it interesting to complete the Executive Presence assessment© at the end of this chapter.

## Generating Opportunity through Visibility

Although it is the twenty-first century, there are still hear grumblings regarding the existence of an "old boys' club." What is this virtual club but a set of people with similar skills, characteristics and common friends, acquaintances and allies? Because the "members" have affiliation through common connections, rapport is gained quickly and it is easier to establish trust, a key component to relationship building. These relationships provide opportunities and can contribute to lucrative introductions.

Although it can feel exclusive when you are on the outside and not an active member of a recognized, powerful, and influential "club" everyone has the capability to create their own strong and valuable network through establishing a large net of alliances and acquaintances.

Amit was a successful senior manager employed with the government in Nova Scotia, Canada. While he enjoyed the lifestyle afforded by the city of less than four hundred thousand people and proximity to the ocean, career opportunities were not as robust as in other major metropolitan centers. After much consideration and conversation with his wife, Amit accepted the role of vice president, regulatory and government relations with a large insurance company and relocated to Toronto.

Although he was well known in the provincial government, when he arrived in Toronto, he had no base of contacts. Five years later, Amit had earned the reputation of being a "connector" someone who regularly introduced friends and colleagues to others in his far-reaching network.

How did he accomplish this? During Amit's first year in in his new city, he joined the board for the Toronto Symphony Orchestra; asked his boss and colleagues for introductions to others with whom he could share and obtain knowledge; offered to speak about government relations at conferences and industry events and he and wife entertained in their home on a regular basis. As Amit was so appreciative of the assistance others provided following his relocation, he wanted to reciprocate and thus developed his reputation for being a connector. It is interesting to note that prior to his relocation, Amit, a natural introvert, was not comfortable in networking situations. Five years later, his base of contacts in Toronto exceeded his Nova Scotia connections.

Amit's success was directly attributable to his purposeful actions and his reciprocity. You can dramatically influence your visibility, greatly multiply your career opportunities and expand your relationships and friendships just as Amit did.

Visibility is equally important when you are already established in an organization. If your expertise is largely in a single domain (e.g., engineering, human resource (HR), or information services (IS)) you may not be well known outside the walls of your organizational silo. However, if you listen large firms—if you are not known—you will not be promoted.

Visibility. A large network. Relationships. They matter. You need them to formulate a strong leadership brand. It is not imperative to join boards or committees or participate in volunteer endeavors but before you rule that out, consider the affiliations you may establish therein.

At the end of this chapter, you will find an example of a relationship map. Creating one can help considerably to put a plan into place.

As you develop more relationships and a larger network, you benefit from gaining greater influence and potentially increased authority. This does not result from connecting with as many people as you can on social media (although social media has benefits that will be explored later). It does not result from simply getting to know a lot of people inside your organization. Visibility results from carefully considering with whom you form relationships with, inside and outside your organization.

Ways to increase your visibility:

- Deliver more than expected. Surprised? Consistently delivering great results gets noticed.
- Suggest improvements. Ideally, make recommendations after you have researched options so that you can demonstrate well thought-out analysis.
- Ask to sit on committees—particularly those that are cross-functional so that you form relationships with people from other departments. Successful ones I have seen include committees for onsite day care; a charity campaign; a facilities move; a diversity committee, and others.
- Offer to make a presentation at a lunch-and-learn session, a town hall meeting, or other corporate gathering.
- If another division provides or receives services from your area or if you have staff who work together, reach out to your peers in that division. Explore what is working well and what challenges they are facing. Perhaps you can jointly identify solutions.
- Consider carefully what you volunteer for. You want to position yourself as being innovative, strategic, knowledgeable, and business focused.

### Expand Your Network

How do you decide whom to build relationships with?

- Who you can offer the greatest assistance to?
- Who is well regarded by others in the organization or industry? You will often discover it is someone who displays executive presence as part of his or her leadership brand.
- Return favors. Make introductions between colleagues and friends you know in other organizations.
- Do you have a mentor? Ask him or her whom you would benefit from meeting. If no mentor, ask your boss, your colleagues, and your friends.

### Integrating into a New Company

If you are new to your organization, identify two to three people that you would like to get to know better. If they are more senior than you are in the organization, it is best to ask for an introduction from your leader or a mentor. Consider the culture of your organization. In some organizations it is frowned upon to approach those in more senior roles unless sanctioned by your boss. Is your boss likely to be sensitive to you speaking to someone more senior without his or her knowledge? If so, first have a conversation with your boss and explain your motives. Ideally they will make some introductions and/or recommend whom you would benefit from meeting with.

## The Power of Brevity

For many years, I considered executive summaries and/or abstracts as analogous to most effective executive interactions. "Be bright. Be brief. Be gone" one of my former leaders used to say. That was a great lesson.

Recently as part of a consulting engagement, I was gathering peer feedback on a CEO. One of his colleagues commented, "He typically uses 300 words to state what could be covered in 50." Obviously, this was not an accolade but an identified area of improvement. Although I am generalizing somewhat, it is important to develop ability to concisely communicate an issue, a recommendation, or an idea. As with all attributes of executive presence, the earlier in your career you do develop this skill, the better.

Executives are bombarded with information. The skillful ones quickly assess and formulate a plan or decision. On a daily basis, like panning for gold, they extract what issues require their attention, what meetings they will attend, what problems carry the greatest risk, what action they must personally take, and what can be delegated to another.

The ability to briefly and effectively communicate will benefit you in all professional interactions. People will pay more attention to what you have to say when you are brief. Your words will carry more weight. Your audience, whether one person or several people, is more likely to retain your message and is more likely to understand your key points if you are brief. This will heighten your influence when communicating.

### Brevity Applies to Meetings

In the world of electronic calendars, meetings have defaulted to sixty-minute durations. The majority of meetings do not require sixty minutes. Eighty percent of my client meetings are less than one hour. Most phone conversations do not require more than fifteen minutes. When I was in executive roles, when I accepted meeting invitations, I typically did so for less time than scheduled. For example, depending on other demands on my time and the subject matter, I would respond to a sixty-minute meeting request by offering my availability for thirty or forty-five minutes.

When meetings are allotted an hour or ninety minutes, the time will be filled. It may not be useful time.

When the meeting time is constrained, you will discover that the most important information will be presented up front; required decisions will be tabled early.

- How can you apply this to the meetings that you chair?
- What changes will you make to the meetings you attend as a participant?

## Judgment

Merriam-Webster defines judgment as an opinion or decision that is on the basis of careful thought or the ability to make good decisions about what should be done. Good judgment forms the foundation for integrity and sound decisions. When you are in a leadership role you are a model, day in and day out, in the office, and in your personal life. Demonstrating sound judgment will engender trust from others and displays strength of character.

> "Steve" was the CEO of a large mining company. Like all commodities industries, the economic verbosity of mining is cyclical and sometimes unpredictable. During a period of economic downturn, Steve enacted a number of difficult financial decisions including staff lay-offs and other expense reductions. He shared the following compass to direct his actions; "I did not make any decisions, or communicate in any way that would not make my mother proud." Another CEO client told me that if he had any hesitancy about a decision being posted the front page of the New York Times, he knew it was the not the right course of action.

## Recovering from Mistakes and Rebuilding Your Reputation

Organizations experience brand damage and the most skillful are able to recover their reputation. Some are not. The Exxon Valdez oil spill occurred in 1989. Well into the twenty-first century, the reputational damage remains. A consumer survey conducted in 2009 ranked Exxon's reputation third to last and respondents mentioned the Valdez spill as the major contributing factor.[1]

Comparatively, following accusations of bribery in 2006, Siemens implemented large-scale changes to its leadership team, processes, and organizational culture.[2] Toyota has faced a variety of product recalls and yet as of 2014 held court as the best-selling car in the United States for more than a decade.[3]

---

[1] http://alisterpaine.com/2009/05/11/exxon-reputation-is-everything/
[2] http://www.mycustomer.com/topic/customer-experience
[3] http://time.com

The year's best-selling car, meanwhile—meaning a sedan, not a truck—was the Toyota Camry, a title the model has held for more than a decade. The official count had it that 408,484 Camrys were sold in the United States in 2013.

Research by the Institute of Business Ethics identified contributors to reputational recovery. The first is the way the company responds to the situation and the second factor is the prior reputation of trustworthiness. So it is with your personal and professional reputation. If you have made a mistake or someone on your team has made an error in judgment or service delivery, you can recover.

- Do not waste any time debating the accuracy of the perception. If others view you unfavorably, accept that perception is reality and move forward.
- Do not make excuses. Do not provide rationale. Do not explain and do not defend.
- Demonstrate humility.
- Take accountability. Admit your error. If it as a result of someone in your department or on your team, take responsibility. You are the leader and the role model. As in all things, all eyes are on you. The impact is on your brand as well as your departments. How you respond to the situation is the key.
- Alter your behavior if necessary and actively demonstrate a (new) brand. If you do not broadly communicate on a regular basis, now is the time to do so. Be visible, particularly to those who have a negative perception. If the error affected your customers, talk to them; visit them; call them. If the situation has altered how your staff or colleagues see you, rebuild your relationships by apologizing (if warranted) and by demonstrating a renewed commitment to doing the right thing.
- If someone on your team or in your division made the mistake, publicly accept responsibility. Make amends. Take disciplinary action if warranted.

## Gender Differences

While I prefer to avoid gender generalizations, as I believe there are as many similarities as differences, I am obliged to share unavoidable obstacles to leadership and personal success. Women are more commonly reported as shy and reticent in business, thus perceived as lacking confidence and/or experience. In spite the growth of women holding senior positions in organizations, stubborn behaviors remain that contribute to these perceptions.

In group settings, capable and intelligent women are less likely to ask questions, particularly provocative questions. I also see them participating less frequently in open discussions, particularly when there are more senior leaders present. At boardroom tables and in meeting rooms, too often, women perch almost tentatively with their notepads or iPads occupying little space on the table. When a room is near or over capacity, sometimes women will even sit at a chair along the wall. This is a big mistake as it acts as an isolator and effectively removes them from the discussion. Sometimes men can fall into the same trap. It inhibits your effectiveness.

Take five minutes following a meeting and ask yourself or a trusted colleague:

- Did I sit at the table in a relaxed and open manner, with my arms uncrossed?
- Did I occupy space at the table—setting out my notepad, electronics, and so on, in front of me or did I tightly pile my items in a small space?
- Did I actively contribute—with at least three questions or observations for every sixty minutes of meeting?
- Did I speak in a way that demonstrated confidence, that is, did I avoid raising my voice at the end of a statement in a way that indicated I was seeking approval or questioning others rather than stating a confident opinion?
- Did I ask provocative questions or make challenging statements or did I hold them inside out of fear of being wrong or offending someone?

- When I offered a differing opinion, did I provide data or examples to support my comment?

> "Patricia" was a highly respected, intelligent executive, commonly known as a high-potential contributor at her law firm. As one of my clients, we discussed developmental feedback she had received from her boss. She and her boss had been speaking quietly in a hallway when a senior partner and founder of the firm stopped to join them. He and her boss started to discuss one of her peers and a sensitive client situation. Patricia felt like she was eavesdropping on information that was not pertinent to her. She unconsciously sought to make herself almost invisible by withdrawing, stepping away slightly and making no comments. The following morning her boss asked her why she had refrained from the conversation. She explained her rationale; she thought she was being respectful. He shared that her silence had a negative effect. She had missed an opportunity to demonstrate her strategic thinking capability and her judgment in a sensitive situation. He encouraged her to speak up, offer recommendations and be an active participant with more senior leaders, particularly when discussing sensitive information. If she did not, over time, she would erode her reputation as a potential senior partner for the firm.

Patricia's boss provided her specific and useful coaching. The coaching provided to Patricia by both her boss and I was to demonstrate the capability for courageous leadership, seize opportunities to heighten her visibility, take actions to enhance her personal brand within the firm, and demonstrate executive presence.

## Leveraging Social Media

Starbucks recognizes the power of social media and have beneficially exploited Twitter, Facebook, and YouTube since 2009. Their massive catchment of customers and fans regularly include Starbucks in their ongoing conversations, further strengthening the brand and deepening customer loyalty.

Use of social media for brand position and marketing is certainly not limited to Starbucks. In a 2013 marketing industry report, eighty-five percent of marketers identified social media as having high value.

When creating and/or furthering your own reputation and brand, the same principles apply. Social media can be a powerful tool.

### LinkedIn

LinkedIn is a great forum with which anyone can build his or her brand—whether gainfully employed or a job seeker.

Create an effective and impactful profile. If you are in an executive role, this is particularly important as your profile corresponds directly back to the company brand. If you are in a more junior role, do not wait until you are considering a career change or are conducting a job search. There are several useful books including *How to Succeed in Business Using LinkedIn* by Eric Butow and Kathleen Taylor or LinkedIn for Dummies. A useful technique for creating your profile is to review profiles of others in your industry and your organization. Make note of the profiles that appear crisp and professional. Review their job summaries to give you ideas. Use a professional photograph. It is a small investment that will heighten your image. Avoid photos with children, dogs, sports gear, and so on. This profile is a reflection of your professional status.

### LinkedIn and Your Employer

If actively employed and enjoying your role in the organization, it can be highly effective to establish yourself as a thought leader. Methods to do this include sharing industry research and trends; writing articles or blog posts. If you are comfortable with public speaking, offer to speak at conferences or association meetings. Topics could include an overview of successful projects or initiatives, successful recruiting or retention tactics, and so on.

Important note: Before you publish any information about your organization, check with your HR department or your manager to familiarize yourself with the corporate standards and practices. You are safe to share public information that has already been disclosed in media releases, the annual report, and so on.

### Making a Career Change

If you are considering a career change or conducting a job search, others will view your profile to augment your resume.

### Leaving a Trail

Social media is a powerful vehicle to augment your reputation. Always consider the uneraseability of information in cyberspace. If in doubt, do not post the comment or information. Although you can always delete information from LinkedIn, Facebook, and other social media sites, it is not fully eliminated from your Internet footprint.

### Building Your Network

Remember as well that your image is enhanced or detracted by the people you associate with. Start by sending invitations to others with whom you already have a business relationship. Get into the habit of making online connections every time you meet people at a conference or social event. When you enter their coordinates into your address book, take a few minutes and send them a LinkedIn invitation.

LinkedIn groups are a popular way to virtually network with others with similar interests. Most organizations have alumni groups and there are groups for every industry and interest.

LinkedIn is a great way to garner introductions to others. If you are seeking an introduction to someone in another organization, look to see whom in your network is connected to that person or others in that organization. You can ask your connection for an introduction.

If you are new to a city or industry, LinkedIn groups can be an effective way to meet others with similar interests and to grow with your knowledge and community. Like in-person networking, you will be most highly regarded if you actively contribute and collaborate. Make introductions to others. Provide suggestions and insights to help others.

### Tips on Building a Powerful Brand

- Corporations understand and exploit brand value. This is one of the reasons that franchises are successful. Consider Gap,

IBM, MacDonald's, Starbucks, Walmart, GE, Apple, and others. Personal brand is equally powerful. You have a brand even if you have not actively created it. Even after only a short time in an organization, you will develop a reputation. You may be seen as someone who gets things done. You may be known as someone who is highly collaborative. The talk in the hallways may be that you keep to yourself and do not openly share ideas. The brand is created with or without your guidance. It is much more powerful to establish how you want to be viewed, to go about creating it and then to check in periodically to assess how others see you.

- What you say may be forgotten by tomorrow. What is on video, in photos, or documented on social media could live much longer than you want it to.
- How long did it take the Dow Jones to drop after a rumor on social media that Barack Obama was ill? Less than sixty seconds. This can be a powerful tool if used well or a hatchet to your reputation and career in no time.
- Understand your company's code of ethics. You will likely be asked to annually confirm that you comply. When in doubt, ask before you act. People have gone to jail for actions that they never expected.
- Meetings are likely to remain a necessary evil for years to come. If you would not pick up a book and start reading it, do not turn on your personal device, smartphone, and so on.
- Be known as a collaborator and a connector. If you are not yet a connector, take the steps identified in this chapter and you can acquire the moniker of connector in a matter of months. Figure 3.1 will help you establish your market presence through networking and building relationships.

Your personal brand and network can be two of your very best assets in managing your career. The information in this chapter helps you to understand the power of your personal brand and the factors that influence your behavior. It also provides actions for expanding and leveraging your network and for identifying what characteristics you want to enhance.

## Network Map
### Lorraine A. Moore Accelerate Success Group 2015

Table 3.1 Buliding a network map

| Name | Company | Strength of Relationship (Strong/Medium/Weak) | Duration of relationship | Commonalities | How can they assist? | How can you assist them? | Who can introduce you? | Action with date |
|---|---|---|---|---|---|---|---|---|
| Sarah Lawrence | Manulife | Strong | 3 years | Industry conference; both MA from Duke; | Introduce me to CEOs in her network in NE | Ask her | N/A | Schedule a conference call before the end of March |
|  |  |  |  |  |  |  |  |  |
|  |  |  |  |  |  |  |  |  |
|  |  |  |  |  |  |  |  |  |

| Fred Jamieson | Starbucks | Weak | N/A | Retail, Board experience | Provide update on status of operations in Italy | Introduce him to other Directors with similar experience | Tim Jorgenson, Starbucks | Call Tim on before Friday Mar 13 |
|---|---|---|---|---|---|---|---|---|
| | | | | | | | | |
| | | | | | | | | |
| | | | | | | | | |
| | | | | | | | | |
| | | | | | | | | |
| | | | | | | | | |
| | | | | | | | | |

# Executive Presence Assessment©

## *Lorraine A. Moore Accelerate Success Group 2015*

**Physical presence:** people described as having executive presence are typically described as: displaying poise, calm, attentive, with good listening skills, an unhurried and confident manner.

**Demeanor:** their behavior is consistent. Their staff and others can anticipate their reactions; therefore, they can be relied upon to respond consistently to challenging situations as well as the day-to-day situation. They demonstrate strategic thinking and operate with a widely communicated vision for the future. They are equally comfortable in social situations and put others at ease.

**Attentive and inspiring:** when people met Jackie Onassis Kennedy, they said that she appeared to listen carefully to their every word. She held eye contact, did not rush conversation and they felt as if she treated them as the only person in the room at that time. She consistently demonstrated attentive presence. Inspiring leaders leave others with renewed belief in their own capabilities and energized about what they can achieve.

*Rate each question:*
 1: Strongly disagree
 2: Disagree
 3: Neither agree nor disagree
 4: Agree
 5: Strongly agree

|  | Rating |
|---|---|
| **Physical Presence**<br>1. I consistently dress as well as or better than the others I am meeting with or presenting with (e.g., with customers, competitors, my leadership team or colleagues, when presenting at community events, presenting on a panel, and so on). |  |
| 2. While perhaps not a fashonista, I maintain good grooming including regular haircuts, clean nails, polished shoes, and so on. |  |
| **Appearance Under Pressure**<br>1. In stressful situations, others would describe me as the calmest person in the room. |  |

|  | Rating |
|---|---|
| 2. When corporate or team results fall short of expectations, I carefully gather facts and confirm or challenge my conclusions before taking action. | |
| 3. The more stressful the situation, the calmer and more pragmatically I lead discussions. | |
| **Attentive Presence** <br> 1. When I am meeting with others I refrain from responding to phone calls, referring to my handheld device, or looking at my computer. | |
| 2. When meeting one-on-one with someone, I listen twice as much as I speak. | |
| 3. I give equal weight and consideration to the opinions of junior staff as I do to the most senior people and external experts. | |
| 4. I ensure meetings begin and end on time and are as efficient as possible. | |
| **Inspiring presence** <br> 1. Others would describe me as inspiring and engaging. | |
| 2. I can accurately portray and describe a compelling vision and optimistic future state. | |
| 3. My direct reports would say that I operate at a strategic level and avoid usurping their responsibilities. | |
| 4. I am proactive with meeting commitments and rarely miss deadlines. | |
| 5. My staff and colleagues would say that they can predict my reactions as my behavior and responses are consistent and predictable. | |

It can be interesting to ask someone else to complete the assessment in addition to completing it yourself. Compare your responses. Where do you see yourself as someone else sees you? Where do you differ?

Is there one area of presence in which you are particularly strong? Is there one area that requires the most attention?

Identify one or two characteristics that you wish to improve. What action(s) will you take to undertake the desired change?

# Courageous Leadership Assessment©

## *Lorraine A. Moore Accelerate Success Group 2015*

The term courageous leadership has been referenced in articles, particularly relating to battle situations. The following assessment incorporates my research and experience.

*Rate each question:*

1: Strongly disagree
2: Disagree
3: Neither agree nor disagree
4: Agree
5: Strongly agree

|   | Rating |
|---|---|
| 1. Others would describe me as the person in the room who will identify and discuss issues or problems, particularly when the subject is sensitive or the opinion may be unpopular. |   |
| 2. I regularly encourage others to challenge my beliefs, biases or views on the company, a sanctioned project, product or service |   |
| 3. I address poor performance, with compassion and respect. I do not avoid the situation hoping it will improve. |   |
| 4. Professional colleagues, friends, and family would all say that I hold myself accountable to a high standard and that I honor my commitments. |   |
| 5. Others would describe me as someone who holds others accountable. I am respectful and unwavering in holding people to account. |   |
| 6. Friends, family, and professional colleagues would say that I demonstrate little reluctance to admitting when I am wrong or have made a mistake. |   |
| 7. I will move forward and make a decision even when others or I have not fully analyzed all available or possible data. |   |
| 8. I have made decisions and taken action when not everyone agreed and/or when not everyone was 100% ready to proceed. This included situations in which there was a risk of failure but for which a successful outcome would benefit customers, employees, or shareholders. |   |

It can be interesting to ask someone else to complete the assessment in addition to completing it yourself. Compare your responses. Where do you see yourself as someone else sees you? Where do you differ?

Whether you complete the assessment independently or with someone else, identify one or two characteristics that you wish to improve. What action(s) will you take to undertake the desired change? Is there a situation to which you can apply a change in your behavior immediately?

# CHAPTER 4

# Excelling at Career Turning Points

Turning points occur at expected and unexpected junctures throughout our professional careers. What I present in this chapter is twofold. In the first half, we examine a structured approach that will help you address some of these turning points—what I call *LEAD490*. In the second half, I consider several unique career junctures that you may face. Accompanying these junctures are many questions, decisions, and possible opportunities of varying complexity. As always, I offer a few narrative scenarios to demonstrate how these tools and situations may evolve.

## LEAD490: Legacy Clarification, Assessment, Data Gathering, Ninety-Day Plan

The LEAD490 model articulates four clear stages to successfully navigate the turning point moments in your career, times when you may be in new circumstances or have critical decisions to make. The qualities of adaptability and direction, discussed in Chapter 3, shape the background against which these career juncture points occur. As you assume more senior leadership positions, these qualities play an even greater role in how you navigate these turning points, since you likely have more at stake—for example, a more deeply established reputation, higher compensation, and personal financial commitments. This model provides a structure for evaluating alternatives.

Turning point junctures arise from several factors, both external and internal. Some of these may be predictable or anticipated. Some will evolve over time. Others may seem to appear out of left field and thus present a shock. Health issues can also precipitate a turning point. Often when people have successfully battled an illness or someone close to them has, they re-evaluate what creates joy in their lives and what they want to make changes.

**External** triggers that may lead to a turning point may include:

Positive:
- a recruiter calls with an opportunity that piques your interest
- you are asked to lead a challenging project at work
- you are offered an opportunity in a different division

Negative:
- a termination through redundancy or other reasons
- a new boss with whom you do not have good chemistry
- organizational restructuring such as management or departmental changes

**Internal** triggers that may lead you to a turning point are:

- you have achieved all you hoped to in your current role and the zeal has evaporated
- you have been in the same job or industry for several years and you are seeking personal and professional growth
- your family situation has changed, resulting in *greater* demands on your personal time, your energy, and your mental focus
- your children have matured and you now find yourself with *more* time and mental energy to direct to your professional life

Whatever the driver, you will encounter turning point moments at various points in your career and life. A differentiator of highly successful leaders is that they respond to these opportunities in well-considered and meaningful ways, contributing to enriched personal and professional lives for both themselves and those who report to them. How do they achieve this? The *LEAD490* Model below will help make this clear.

## Legacy Clarification

Closely aligned with direction, your legacy statement helps define your intentions for your career and overall life. I always envision this quasi-vision as a lighthouse on the edge of a craggy shore. Its light shines in the distance so that the entire structure becomes visible as you approach the shore. The best legacy plans are emotional and aspirational. They define the essence of a fulfilled career for a period of time and they generate anticipation and excitement within you.

When artfully creating one's life vision, my most successful clients consider the full spectrum of their personal and professional lives and as such, we begin by imagining a bright future, with all aspects aligned in harmony.

This is the cornerstone to a successful career. The many successful leaders I work with revisit the following exercise every few years, particularly when making a change or course correction. As you complete this, let your imagination flow.

> ### Exercise 1 – Project five years out
>
> - How would you feel if you were in the same job? Sitting in the same office?
> - Would you like to be working at the same company?
> - Why or why not?
> - What about location? If you work for a global or national organization, is mobility an important factor for promotion?
> - If so, have you worked in other locations? If not, have you talked to your boss about how soon you should move to demonstrate your willingness to do so?
> - Have you talked to him or her regarding options and locations?
> - What other jobs are appealing to you?
> - What aspects of those jobs interest you?

Now we turn to the nearer term and hold a mirror to your future self. In your imagination, place yourself twenty-four and thirty-six months out. As you complete the exercise below, consider these questions:

If someone observed you for a day at each of these times, what would they see? If that person were to speak to your colleagues, direct reports, leader, or others, what words would they hear being used to describe you?

What will success look like when you review the metrics for your operation, department, or sales team at each of these points?

> ## Exercise 2 – Draft your legacy statement
>
> Identify three to five words that each of the following stakeholders will ideally use to describe you in two to three years:
> - Customers
> - Employees
> - Colleagues in the organization
> - Suppliers
> - Your board

Identify two to five quantitative measures of success.

Referencing examples below, draft your legacy statement.

> Sample legacy statements:
>
> "By spring 2015, our customers will herald our sales team as the most responsive and client-focused professionals they have ever worked with. The Operations Team will recognize our team as being highly collaborative and respectful."
>
> "Within 3 years we will deliver this $10B project on time, on budget, and with no reportable safety incidents. The project team will consider this the most exciting project they have worked on in their careers. We will be interviewed and featured in *Fortune Magazine*."
>
> "We will have dramatically improved the relationships between our suppliers and my division. We will have reduced operating costs by ten percent. We will hold a joint celebration with our suppliers in Orlando."
>
> "By 2016 we will have been selected as one of Canada's best-managed companies. Employee engagement will be at an all-time high. Customer satisfaction will exceed ninety percent and we will have no serious safety incidents."

A legacy statement can also be particularly useful when you are experiencing an internal turning point—when you are feeling dissatisfied and are seeking a new challenge. Crafting the legacy statement can bring clarity to your thoughts and help formulate appropriate actions so that you can then move forward. To be adaptable in our personal and professional lives, we benefit from an overarching direction and life trajectory.

## Assessment

We may feel pressured to take action in the first several weeks of accepting a new role. This can be a self-imposed pressure or an overt expectation from our boss, the board, or others. It may be exacerbated if financial results are poor or if there are issues with employee morale, customer satisfaction, or financial results. However, moving quickly to action does not necessarily produce sustainable, positive benefits.

Even in situations where decisions must be taken to address financial issues, product quality problems, employee retention, and so on, the most effective leaders understand the importance of careful assessment. Before leaping into action, highly effective leaders use all of their senses to first observe and learn—this is the core of assessment. By not immediately mobilizing into action, pragmatic leaders allow themselves time to validate and assess their first impressions. Because leaders in new roles have not yet acclimatized to their new context, they can see the issues facing their organization with a fresh set of eyes.

If you are in a new leadership role, the initial period of 90 to 120 days is a great time to rapidly make numerous observations: the opportunities for improvement, systemic issues, long-standing grudges, political posturing, and so on. Observing, asking questions, and listening—before cementing a plan—will engender greater support for any changes you implement. Since successfully executing your plans relies on the support of your team, department, or division, the understandings you collect during this early stage lay the groundwork for your success.

The challenge here is this: depending on the seniority of your role and/or the organizational culture, new leaders—which could be you—often feel they are expected to deliver results very quickly, rather than taking the time they need to really acclimatize to the state of affairs. Furthermore, most leaders in new roles want to demonstrate that they are the right person for the job and experience an internal propensity for action.

I advise my clients to identify and, where possible, immediately resolve employee, customer, or board concerns. In parallel to this, they must take time to observe–to assess—the broader landscape.

> "Susan" accepted a leadership role in the corporate head office. Her five-hundred-plus employees were spread over ten locations across the country. Much like a Dilbert cartoon, her staff spent their workdays in rows of cubicles. Within the first sixty days, she visited each location and walked the floors, observing and eliciting feedback. She quickly discovered that the work environments were not ideal. There was insufficient natural light and many of the desks and chairs were decades old.
>
> Within six weeks, she ordered replacement office furniture and changed the layout in several locations, allowing outdoor light to penetrate the work areas. This simple change had powerful results in employee productivity and job satisfaction. At the same time, it had little or no long-term negative implications for the organization, so it could be acted upon early.

---

### Exercise 3 – Find room for improvement

Look at three situations; identify three opportunities for improvement.

*Observe:*
   Examples are: team meetings, town hall meetings, on-site meetings with customers, plant or field tours, and staff meetings.

*Ask questions:*
   Gather information from at least three stakeholder groups to get a variety of perspectives for a more complete picture. Examples are: direct reports, customers, suppliers, analysts, consultants, colleagues in other departments, your boss, and the Board.

> *Make notes:*
> - What are the common themes?
> - How long has this problem existed?
> - How urgent is a solution to the problem?
> - Which items require your action and which ones can you delegate to people on your team?
> - What practices have you seen elsewhere that might work here?
> - What is the cost of resolving the issues? What are the benefits?
> - Do you have the authority to implement necessary changes or must you collaborate with others (HR, other colleagues, or the board)?
> - What problems are affecting employee engagement?
>
> *Synthesize:*
> What actions can you take in the first weeks to demonstrate that you heard and are acting on others' feedback?

## Data Gathering

The best leaders combine their observations, intuitive reactions, judgment, and active listening with quantitative data—facts, trends, statistics, and hard results. Because you aspire to be the best leader possible, this is a skill you must demonstrate. Quantitative data can be gathered from a variety of sources, including your company's annual report; stock price over time; corporate, divisional and department budgets and expenses; balanced scorecards; employee engagement scores; employee turnover and average tenure statistics; and more.

It is also highly beneficial to gather external information and benchmarks to compare and contrast with the internal results. Sources of external comparators will vary depending upon your industry, geography, and organizational responsibilities. Best sources of this information include: industry peers, associations, research organizations such as Forrester Research, Gartner Inc., Catalyst, McKinsey, and others, as well as suppliers.

Reading publications such as The Economist, New York Times, The Wall Street Journal, and others will keep you abreast of trends across industry and throughout the world. The Internet also offers a wealth of information, but I remind you to consider the credibility of the source.

Ensure that you compare internal and external statistics to the anecdotal information provided to you. Judge and measure them both against your own conclusions. This is just as important when you have been in a role for several years. You can also use this information to formulate your questions for others. By referencing this quantitative information when communicating with others, you can gather support for the changes you are undertaking. Data also enables you to validate your findings.

> ## Exercise 4 – Gather data
>
> *If you are new to the organization*, review the annual report, analyst reviews, press releases, and other public information. What jumped out at you? What trends did you identify?

*Read* the company strategy, values statements, and defined leadership behaviors. What did you learn? Did anything surprise you?

*Observe* behaviors. Are the leadership and employees behaving in ways that are consistent with the espoused strategies and corporate priorities?

*Investigate* employee engagement scores. How does your department compare with overall company results? Are you gaining or losing market share? What can you glean from the customer satisfaction scores and comments?

*Review* service level agreements—for services that you are providing to customers or internally to other departments and divisions. Are the agreements being met? Do they cover all areas of service delivery? What questions do you have?

*Study* all department and divisional metrics. A department scorecard can be enlightening, if you can access this. Where is your team performing well?

*Identify* the gaps that you discover.

*Note* what opportunities you believe will provide the greatest return?

*Speak* with others. Are your observations consistent with others? Will your feedback and recommendations be readily accepted and/or an unwelcome surprise?

## Ninety-Day Plan

Ideally, before the end of the first month in a new leadership position you will create a ninety-day plan (see Table 4.1 for an example). If you are in a senior role, perhaps a multiyear strategic plan is in order and if so, should be completed within the first six months. As with clarifying your legacy, a ninety-day plan will release you from the shackles of "being busy" and free you to become a results-oriented leader. Its power lies in its simplicity. The plan incorporates work, family, and personal commitments. Making it public will increase your likelihood of sticking to it, so deliberately share it with your team and colleagues.

Here is a sample ninety-day plan:

Table 4.1 Legacy statement: *My three most important objectives this quarter*

| | | | |
|---|---|---|---|
| • January | • Schedule interviews with each new direct report<br>• Create my legacy statement and ask each of my leadership team to create their own | • Spend every Sunday with Joanne and the kids—no work | • Call personal trainer to sign up again for weekly check-ins |
| • February | • Review all internal reports and contracts with key suppliers<br>• Schedule meetings with key business partners | • Offer to assist at Glen's hockey practices | • Read at least one book for pleasure |
| • March | • Hold first employee town hall<br>• Ask each of my leaders to showcase their team's accomplishments | • Book summer holiday<br>• Research kids' summer camps | |

Many types of situations will occur over the course of your working life. Some of these will be calls to action; others will be calls for reflection and adjustment. You will find that both adaptability and direction will inform the paths you take as you encounter these various events and that LEAD490 will be a useful tool to negotiate this terrain.

### Newly Promoted

> "Paul" became a director in an oil company's engineering department, a managerial role that he felt he needed assistance with. He wished to achieve the objectives for the first twelve months, while developing relationships with his new teams and planning for the next five years. This left him with quite a few different balls to keep in the air simultaneously.
>
> Paul wanted to make a great first impression on the executive team, his colleagues, and his staff. This would be a tall order, because within days of starting this new job, he had to provide a plan to restructure his new team and reduce costs by twenty percent. He was not sure how best to achieve this, knowing he was going to be making some potentially unpopular decisions.

Over the next six months, I coached Paul as he followed my *LEAD490* model to create a highly effective and executable plan. Paul thought carefully about his values, his experience, and the contribution he wanted to make as a director. We created a plan that enabled his team to participate in the cost-reduction exercise while maintaining his role as the final decision maker and ensuring that he was able to meet the imposed deadlines. He identified the three most important priorities for his first year and sought his leader's confirmation. I assisted him in creating a road map of tasks for the first eighteen months that included identifying critical milestones. Every two weeks, we assessed his progress against the three key goals and these milestones. Whenever Paul detoured to attend to other seemingly important tasks, I rerouted him back to the most significant, previously agreed to priorities.

When I checked in with him two years later, he was enjoying his job immensely. He had learned a great deal, was highly respected by his teams, and his department was exceeding every service metric. Paul demonstrated the aforementioned adaptability and direction necessary to achieve this success. At least once each year, he reviewed his five-year plan in the form of his legacy statement. Every quarter, he updated his ninety-day plan and evaluated his progress for the previous quarter. He made adjustments where necessary and appropriate. He maintained discipline while willingly adjusting his course as corporate priorities or personal demands necessitated. This balance of discipline and adaptability are hallmarks of successful professionals.

## Changing Industries

> "Alicia" was a successful finance executive. Having worked for many years in the transportation industry, she was CFO of a regional airline. When a competitor acquired her company, she recognized that she had a unique opportunity before her. The merged organization would require only one CFO. The CEO and Board could choose to keep her or select the acquiring organization's CFO. Although she wanted to remain in the same city for personal reasons, she began to consider other industries. While she had greatly enjoyed her time at the airline, she wondered if she could transfer her skills to a new industry.

Following the *LEAD490* model, Alicia started by reviewing her legacy plans. She had a defined yet flexible direction for her life that included contributing to her employer's success, maintaining a deep involvement with her family, and continuing with volunteer work. This contributed to her choice to remain in her metropolitan center. She was confident that her skills and financial acumen equipped her well for senior finance roles.

As soon as the acquisition was public knowledge, Alicia commenced her data gathering by reaching out to her broad network and also to recruiting firms. She researched industries to identify those with forecast growth and head office locations in her city. She updated her resume to highlight her transferrable skills in governance, due diligence, financial analysis, and other areas.

As she gathered more introductions and received positive feedback from others regarding her abilities and marketability, she also advised her CEO and the Board, that she would leave the organization at the completion of the merger. Although somewhat risky, this allowed her to align her behavior with her values of transparency and integrity. She was able to openly and actively pursue other employment options while fully contributing to the success of her firm during the transition.

The outcome: she successfully secured a CFO role with a credit union. The Board and CEO of the financial institution were particularly impressed during the interview process with the six- and twelve-month plans that she created for the potential role.

Part of Alicia's success in networking and data gathering resulted from her consistently offering to help others by making introductions, recommending books and articles, and sharing ideas. In this way, she strengthened her reputation and increased the size of her network. She drew on the expertise of others in her first year at the credit union and used best practices she had observed in the airline industry.

### *Other Career Turning Points*

The financial services industry has sought to educate us on the benefits of asset diversification. Rather than placing all of our investments in one company's stock, one industry, or one country, we are better protected from the ups and downs of individual economies through a diversified portfolio. Managing your career is very much like this. Many transition points will come your way, which you can watch slide by or actively respond to. My bias is to identify and seize the opportunities presented to you through transition. Doing so forms the basis of a much richer life.

*LEAD490* is a proven tool that works well for many people actively engaging such key transitional points in their careers. To further enhance your capabilities in responding to other possible turning points, we will consider a variety of additional potential opportunities and decision points that may present themselves along on your lengthy career path. You may also find these an excellent reference when mentoring others faced with turning points.

## Playing It Safe Versus Remaining Challenged

In an earlier section, I highlighted the sometimes-prerequisite breadth of experience required to achieve a senior executive role, particularly in large organizations. The same is true for creating true job "security." In the mid-1900s, people were rewarded for staying with one organization for their entire careers, aiming for retirement and the clichéd gold watch. That world has long departed. Statistics Canada reports that just 38.8 percent of employees had an employer-sponsored pension plan in 2010, down from forty-five percent in 1991. This trend, among other factors, has contributed to most North Americans working for a variety of employers over their career life. Job security is now obtained by regularly and consistently improving your capabilities and the value you deliver to any employer.

> While bored and unchallenged at work, "Louise" enjoyed the good compensation and flexible work hours afforded by her role as a Senior Vice President, Compliance. In her city of three hundred thousand people, there were a dozen or so very good professional employers, the majority of them in the manufacturing or retail sectors. She had been in her current senior management role for ten years. She could predict the annual cycles of budget planning and performance management, as well as the months of high volume customer demands.
>
> She and her managers had identified and dealt with all possible process improvements, and she was riding a wave of competence, predictability, and comfort. She was then offered an interesting and challenging opportunity to turn around a division with poor employee morale and customer satisfaction. She politely declined, as she did not really want to contribute the extra effort that she believed would be required in the new role.

When we met, I advised Louise that she was trending toward a crash as she had lost her edge. She was no longer challenged: she was no longer seeing opportunities for further improvement and, therefore, she was not innovative. Her myopic view resulted in her approaching "the same problems with the same solutions" even when they were not necessarily the same underlying business problems. Her organization gave careful consideration to talent development and succession planning. In their assessment, she fit the profile of a "blocker." She had occupied a senior role for longer than was ideal, making it unavailable to others as a growth and development opportunity.

Even if the organization enabled her to stay in her current role for another five years or more, what then? Her boredom would eventually outweigh the enjoyment of her unchallenging position. By that time, even if she wanted to make a move, her skills would have atrophied compared to others who had continued to develop and challenge themselves professionally. The other possibility was that eventually the organization would offer her an alternative and undesirable position. Her "choice" would be between accepting it and leaving the company.

Playing it safe, as Louise had been doing, increases your risk. Lack of flexibility can have serious consequences for your career. You will attain the greatest job security through continual mastery of the skills in your profession—whether these are technical expertise, leadership, or relationship management skills. This demonstrated business acumen combined with an overall career plan, which will enable you to adapt to externally imposed changes along with any opportunities you actively seize.

## International Assignments

Many multinational organizations consider international assignments to be a prerequisite for senior executive roles. When managers work in a variety of offices and locations, they can contribute to a stronger corporate culture by sharing values and best practices. International experience is considered beneficial to broaden cultural awareness and expand one's global thinking. This is particularly common with organizations that sell their products and/or services to a variety of markets.

Is an expatriate assignment right for you? When assisting my clients in evaluating international assignment options, I encourage them to review their overall life plan and trajectory, as well as their career interests and personal commitments. Consider if it is the best or near-best timing for you and your family, and if it aligns to your goals. If you determine this is appropriate for you, seize the opportunity. You will grow personally and professionally through the experience and will further your adaptability to changing life experiences.

### *Exploring International Assignments*

- What is driving you to consider this?

- Is this a lifestyle choice? For example, have you previously enjoyed living abroad or traveling extensively?
- Is this a career-path choice that is consistent with your direction?
  - Do you work at or intend to work at a multinational organization?
  - Are you aspiring to a C-suite role where this is leverage or is required?
- How does this fit with your overall life plan?
  - Do you have few commitments in your personal life such that you have freedom?
  - If you have a spouse or partner, how does this fit with their life and career goals?
  - Can your partner obtain a work visa and/or otherwise work in the locations you are considering?
  - If not, will this create conflict?
- How long do you anticipate living abroad?
- How large are the cultural differences?
- Do you require or would you benefit from a second language?
- Have you spoken with others who have taken international assignments?
  - What was their biggest surprise?
  - Did they achieve the career benefits they were seeking?

## Taking a Sabbatical or Leave of Absence

Sabbaticals have long been common in academia. Professors often take sabbaticals to conduct research, further their thought leadership, or to author a book. In the past several years, more people in a career context are taking sabbaticals or leaves of absences too. Many factors may lead to such an occurrence—some are driven by the individual's desires and others are the result of a company-based change, such as one's position being made redundant. As we have discussed, adapting to unexpected moments and seizing opportunities is a measure of a successful career. Perhaps a sabbatical or leave of absence is part of that picture.

Sometimes individuals actively pursue a sabbatical, having identified the need for personal or professional renewal. Some organizations have formalized programs in which you can defer twenty percent of your salary every year for five years with the understanding that you will take the sixth year as a sabbatical. Even organizations that do not typically offer sabbaticals are often supportive of a leave of absence of a few months, particularly if you choose to be away during a slower business cycle. If the plan for your life includes travel, study, adventure, or fresh experiences, a sabbatical or leave of absence could be a wise option.

Once you've done your homework by assessing the above factors and have made a decision to request a leave, it is time to discuss your intention with your boss. Many factors come into play here. Ask yourself these questions:

## Exercise 5 – Assess your options

- Does your organization offer sabbaticals or leaves of absence?
  - *YES:* Research the options before speaking with your boss.
  - *NO:* Do you know anyone in the company who has taken a leave? Ask for a confidential meeting to discuss their experience and recommendations.
- Have you been with your company for three years or more?
  - *YES:* Ideally you have established a great track record and have made a continuous contribution. Perhaps the time is right.
  - *NO:* Give this option more time, so that you can really demonstrate your value to the company before making this request.
- Are your performance ratings acceptable?
  - *YES:* Your performance "meets expectations" or better yet, "exceeds expectations."
  - *NO:* You have yet to ensure that you have fulfilled your obligations.
- What is the purpose of your leave?
  - *YES:* You are pursuing further education, will be participating in a charitable initiative such as building

> a school in a developing country, or your assistance is required for elder care. Be prepared to clearly articulate your rationale and how the company will benefit upon your return, if applicable.
>   - *NO:* You are bored, feeling burned out, are not sure you want to remain with your employer, or do not know what your next role should be. Research your options within the organization. Revisit the LEAD490 model and update your five-year view. Update your ninety-day plan to research options. Reach out to a mentor or a trusted friend.
> - How will you fund your leave? The longer you plan to be away from work, the more important this becomes.
>   - Will you direct part of your pay to savings for a period of time prior to taking the leave?
>   - Can you sublet your home during your absence, to provide a stream of income?
> - What about benefits coverage?
>   - Some organizations will continue benefits coverage during an approved leave, but you may need to pay up front.

- *Do you expect your immediate boss to be supportive?* If not, you will need to adequately prepare for the discussion and be prepared to accept a shorter duration of leave or to be declined.
- *Consider the professional risk you may be taking.* This may be shaped by how typical or not such a leave is in your organization. If your leave is declined, will your employer view you as less committed to the organization and/or to your career? If this is possible, it could limit your opportunities for promotion and even compensation. This does not mean you need to toss away your desire for a leave, but you need to first think carefully about your priorities. If this is your situation

and the driving force is to take a leave, be prepared that you may need to find another employer upon your return.
- *How much notice will you give your employer?* If you are planning to take one year, I recommend giving six to nine months' notice. If you are going to take two to three months, then two months' notice is likely sufficient.

Remember, your boss may need to explain or defend his or her decision to colleagues, the Board, or other affected parties, particularly if such leaves are not common in your company. Also, if approved for you, your boss is setting a precedent they need to consider for others. It will be easier for your leader to approve the request if you:

- Provide a meaningful rationale for the leave and plenty of notice.
- Quantify any and all benefits to the organization.
  - If your team can operate without you during your absence, this will be a cost savings to the company.
  - Recommend someone to fill in during your absence (backfilling). This provides a developmental opportunity and less risk to the company than leaving your position vacant.
- Agree to make yourself occasionally available during your absence for remote communications. You could offer to check e-mail once every week or two or agree to otherwise check in.
- Negotiate the duration, timing, or other factors of the leave. This may be easier if you are not attending an academic program where scheduling is less flexible.

## Pursuing Further Education

Many of my mid-career clients seek my opinion on further education. This is particularly true of those with deep technical expertise such as physicians, pharmacists, engineers, geologists, and others. Continuous and constant professional development is imperative. Formal education is one option.

"Craig" was a senior manager at a large retail company. At the age of thirty-five he had spent much of his career with the same company and had secured progressively more senior roles in Supply Chain. He aspired to executive roles in the organization and wondered if he would benefit from pursuing an MBA. In his personal life, his children were in elementary school and active in sports. His wife also had an active and demanding job.

In Craig's case, we determined that it was an opportune time for him to complete an executive MBA through an international university. In reviewing his overall life direction, he identified his priorities as: achieving a global assignment, gaining experience beyond Supply Chain, maintaining leisure time with friends and family, and valuing the pursuit of learning. As his children were active in school and extracurricular activities, a part-time and online MBA would allow him time to attend some of their events. Furthermore, upon graduation, his children would still be in elementary school, so an international assignment might be more feasible from the family perspective sooner rather than later, before his kids became teenagers.

By selecting an international school, he would be exposed to other cultures and global organizations, while acquiring the general knowledge of business that is part of an MBA. This was important, as Craig's expertise was largely limited to Supply Chain. This would better qualify him to work in other divisions of the organization.

Is further education suitable for you?

- You enjoy learning and/or reading.
- You have a keen interest in learning more, and additional study offers you the appropriate subject matter (e.g., Masters in Leadership, Masters in Business, and Masters in Health).
- You will be able to dedicate twenty to thirty hours per week to school (for masters programs).
- You want to make a significant career change, (e.g., from banking to health care) and the education will increase your marketability, expand your network, and give you the required skills.

- Your partner is supportive, and is willing and able take on the extra load that will be created in your "absence" due to studying, writing assignments, meeting with study groups, and so on.
- You can pay for the program, or your employer will fund some or all of it.

### *Part time or Full time?*

In my own case, before commencing my Masters I researched a number of options and seriously considered a full-time program. After careful consideration, I opted for an online, part-time program with three weeks of residence/classes. This worked well for me as it meant a schedule flexible enough to accommodate my work travel demands and for me to attend my children's soccer games and be at the dinner table much of the time.

I was working for a Canadian bank at the time and observed that all senior colleagues pursuing their MBA had selected the executive MBA/part-time option. This enabled them to remain active in their role and in the organization. I should point out, however, that when I embarked on my MBA, a wise mentor advised me to be prepared that no matter how supportive my spouse said he would be, I should understand there would be times he would regret that he ever said that! I was fortunate that he was indeed very supportive for the two-plus years of my program—but do not forget that it is a big commitment for your partner too.

Many part-time programs allow students up to seven years to complete the degree, should they wish to take breaks along the way. In the end, even if you work straight through, knowing you have flexibility will provide peace of mind.

### *Part time and/or Online?*

Consider the following points as you assess what may be the best modality for you:

- You are self-disciplined enough to complete assignments on a sunny day or to defer social activities when required.

- You want or need to maintain an income stream.
- You are well established in your career and the opportunity cost of leaving the workforce for one to two years outweighs the benefits.
- You want to apply the learning to your workplace immediately.
- You would like to use a real situation from your organization for your thesis or other projects. (You will need to obtain permission from your employer. Some organizations are very supportive and others do not allow this for confidentially and competitive reasons.)
- Your employer may fund part of or your entire program if you agree to remain with the organization for a specified length of time following graduation.

### *What about Accreditations?*

Early in your career, accreditations can be particularly useful, or at times when you are making a career change. Some of the following programs may be appropriate:

- Project Management Professional (PMP) has a positive long-standing reputation and is a requirement for most senior project manager roles across all industries.
- Accreditations in Human Resources (CHRP) are also common and largely expected for HR management roles.
- Other designations such as IIBA (Business Analyst) or Prosci (Change Management) may be useful in augmenting your experience, but do not offer the same leverage and clout as post-graduate programs or the PMP.

### *Executive Programs*

If you are a director, assistant vice president, or vice president, your organization may sponsor you to attend an executive program. This is an excellent opportunity for learning, networking, and expanding your knowledge and capabilities. Most North American colleges offer executive programs in Finance, Leadership, Strategy, and Operations, as well as other related areas. These are often excellent programs with highly skilled faculty members. There are both residence programs and shorter duration courses. If you are a senior or executive vice president in a Fortune 500 company or a C-suite role in a mid-cap firm and have not completed an MBA, it can be highly beneficial to attend an intensive, accelerated MBA-type program. Harvard and other reputable schools offer programs that are typically nine months in duration. This will provide you with access to senior professionals across industry and affords you an opportunity to remain connected to your workplace while completing the program.

### *Setting the Course for Your Career and Life*

The most successful executives with a balanced and fulsome career and personal life, embrace an overall direction for their lives and careers while demonstrating adaptability in response to exciting opportunities, unexpected challenges, and changes within their work or personal life. This section has provided a set of tools that you can use to address emergent situations or assess potential situations. When encountering opportunities or facing a crossroads in your life, only you can determine the right choice for yourself. The key to sustained career success and a seat at the executive table is an evolving life direction and the willingness to alter your course and seize opportunities as they presented themselves. Turning points are intrinsic to this journey.

# CHAPTER 5

# Multifaceted Leadership

In this chapter, we will explore different facets of leadership and how to successfully navigate a variety of challenges. We will explore what it means to model personal accountability and how to hold others to account.

## Debunking the Four-Hour Work Week

Tim Ferriss' popular book, *The Four-Hour Work Week,* suggests that we can cast off the chains of servitude to our employers and live a life of adventure—hiking, skiing, and diving at glorious destinations around the globe. Although I agree with Tim that many of us can be considerably more productive in our work, leadership requires your presence and contribution on a consistent basis. Our employees want and need access to us and, in many cases, so do our customers. While you may be able to work part time or undertake an alternative work option (explore this idea further in Chapter 2, *Establishing a Career Without Sacrificing a Life*) leadership roles require an investment of time and energy that often exceed a forty-hour work week.

As this book is targeted to the hundreds of thousands of leaders in companies of all sizes, how can you maintain a high level of productivity and lead others to achieve the same?

Bureaucratic environments rely on structure, process, and consistency. These mechanisms enable predictability and reliability, but can also stifle innovation. Start-ups and technology companies in Silicon Valley long ago challenged our beliefs that all companies have to operate with traditional dress codes, work hours, organization structures, titles, and hierarchy. Consider the culture at Google and similar enterprises.

If you are a Fortune 500-sized organization, it is possible and may be preferable for your executives to create meaningful microcultures that enable flexibility and respond to the market or other factors while adhering to overall company values and to the nonnegotiable practices enforced by regulatory requirements and labor laws.

There are varying degrees of wastes in every company. There is a correlation between larger companies and more waste. As your company grows, you introduce more process and strive for greater consistency. This is beneficial, but there is a point of diminishing returns. As time passes, processes that were created to address past gaps are no longer required, as technology, product, or service changes have eliminated the gap. However, in many cases, this is not recognized. The employee who created the original process in response to the gap or reporting requirement has moved on to a new role. The current incumbents are doing the job as they were trained to do.

I have heard a funny and analogous story that illustrates this. I am not able to credit the source but here it is. . . A practiced cook always removed some of the meat off both sides of a beef roast before preparing it. Her husband asked her why she did this. She said she thought it improved the flavor or the cooking process, but she was not sure. What she did know was that her mom always cut the ends off the Sunday dinner roast beef before putting it in the oven. She called her mother to ask why that improved the flavor of the roast. Her mom responded, "Oh, I don't do that anymore. I used to do that when you were young because the roasting pan was too small and often the roast was too long to fit in the pan." So it is at our workplaces.

## Harnessing Productivity

In Chapter 9, Elevating Results through Innovation, we will explore methods to identify and eliminate redundant activities. Here are practical steps to achieve the important balance of structure and efficiency. You will not reduce your workweek to four hours, but you and your team can take much more control over your time and achieve more in fewer hours.

1. First, establish and communicate your strategy and the divisional and departmental goals (see Chapter 6, Harnessing Performance).

2. Establish and document the most important goals and key performance indicators for each of your direct reports (Chapter 6).
3. Next, through discussion with your direct reports, identify their unique characteristics. This will help to formulate their development plan and your succession planning (Chapter 7, Talent for the twenty-first Century).

> Many years ago, one of my best performers was the biggest offender for arriving late at the office. When she was at work, she was heads down, focused, reliable, and had the capacity to push through large volumes of work (some of her unique characteristics). She was consistently in the office when others left for the day as she really gained her second wind in the late afternoon. After a few conversations about her tardiness with her giving a commitment to be on time more often, I started to wonder if we were taking the wrong approach.
>
> Her projects consistently met budget and exceeded schedule. Her team and stakeholders respected her. She did not have a family or other morning demands; her energy levels and biorhythms were simply such that it was very difficult for her to arrive and to be alert before 8:30 a.m. We took a different approach.
>
> We scheduled project meetings and daily stand-up meetings for 9 a.m. or later. We refrained from conversations about arriving by 8 a.m. and instead sought her expertise on how to elevate the performance of other project teams to equal that of hers. This took pressure off everyone—from me for having Groundhog Day conversations that were not resulting in the desired change and from her on several fronts. Her appreciation was considerable and the company retained a high-performing project manager for many years. This delivered results right to the bottom line.

4. Create fit for purpose reward and recognition practices that are aligned to your strategic objectives.
    - In sales-focused organizations like CISCO or SAP, reward and recognition programs are typically well established and formalized. This is also the case in some retail companies like

McDonalds or GAP. Whether or not formal programs exist, you can achieve tremendous return on investment (ROI) through small methods of reward and recognition.

> One of my clients was facing tough competitive challenges. A long-standing successful company, they had not released any new products in over five years. Employees and leaders had become somewhat complacent. The Vice President, Marketing wanted to emulate the creative nature of a start-up. She launched an internal campaign to identify possible new products. She created a review board comprised of people from all across the company. With created friendly competitions across departments and different office locations, she granted individual and team rewards.
>
> All corporate reward mechanisms such as performance bonuses, etcetera remained in place. The nine-month product innovation launch was an adjunct and was a huge success. They received over forty great ideas and launched three groundbreaking new products before year-end.

5. Establish and adhere to efficient and productive practices. Simplicity is the secret ingredient of productivity practices that will be sustained.
   - Write down the three actions you will complete before anything else each day. Yes, I know you likely have sixteenth to twenty priorities on your to-do list at any given time. Get over it. Pick 3 ☺
   - Pareto's 80/20 rule applies here. Twenty percent of your activities will contribute to eighty percent of your results. Without discipline and persistence, many people first complete several of the small tasks on their list because the three most important items are often more onerous, time-consuming, or require a greater investment of your time and energy.
   - Your top three items may require you to engage and influence others who are resistant. They rarely deliver immediate results and therefore lack immediate gratification.
   - Some examples of top three items that I often see delayed are:

- A performance management conversation with a direct report who is not meeting expectations or taking the required steps to replace the individual.
- Crafting key messages that you will deliver to the company or your division or department about an impending change or difficult decision such as a plant closure or expense reductions.
- A difficult conversation with a peer who you expect will be resistant to your suggestions, feedback, or conversation about his/her department not meeting your expectations.
- A discussion with a peer or direct reports where there is conflict resulting from a lack of role clarity.
- Meeting with a dissatisfied client.
- In each of these cases, today's action will not completely resolve a situation but it will contribute to improved performance over time. That is why these are the actions you must address before any taking action on other tasks.
- Create your list every morning or, even better, before end of day each day for the following day.
- Stick to it. If you have scheduled a conference call or meeting for the start of your day, you either need to start your day earlier or move the meeting or conference call. Holding your own feet to the fire can be more difficult than holding others to account, however, the payback is large and sustained. You are a role model for others and every day you take actions contributing to company viability and performance.

Meeting-it is most common for middle management staff. Most executives understand the importance of attending to strategic priorities. As well, demands on their time and travel schedules often mean that they are less likely to be pulled into as many meetings. If you are an executive leader, model your process for deciding which meetings you will attend with your staff and ask them to report on the changes they are making to their meeting attendance.

If you are in a middle management role, I expect you find yourself in back-to-back meetings and conference calls with no allocated time for washroom breaks or elevator transfer.

Here are some immediate ways to change that:

- Pick up the phone instead of responding to or sending an e-mail—at least three times every day.
- Accept one-hour (or longer) meetings only on an exception basis. Many of my clients have benefited from this practice.
  - Outlook calendar is wonderful for organizing our work and personal lives, however, similar to all technology, it is a double-edged sword. The pervasive use of electronic calendars has defaulted us to setting almost every meeting for a minimum of one hour.
  - Change your default to thirty minutes. Advise the meeting organizer that you are available for only thirty minutes. When you are requesting a meeting, keep it to thirty minutes. Then start on time, even if not everyone is in attendance. End on time, even if not everyone (including you) shared his or her viewpoint.
  - When I was a corporate executive, if I arrived at a meeting and the required others were not there, I would wait five to seven minutes. Then before returning to my office, I would then write on the white board, "I was here at 10 and left at 10:05." This quickly altered the habitual meeting tardiness.
  - Here are the wonderful outcomes of these steps: if the attendees require your approval or want to advise you of an urgent issue, they will ensure that this is communicated early in the allotted time. People are much more likely to arrive on time as they do not want to miss anything. Everyone gains thirty minutes that previously would have been spent in a meeting room or on a conference call with no additional ROI for the additional investment of time.
  - Similarly, reduce ninety-minute meetings to sixty minutes and two-hour meetings to ninety minutes.
- Do not repeat information or "catch up" anyone who arrives late to the meeting. They can review presentations, read documented action items, and/or speak with someone offline.

You do not want to reward the wrong behavior and be seen to penalize those who arrive on time.
- Do not fall into the trap of organizing a follow-up meeting to bring up to speed those who were absent. This is a common and insidious practice in companies that have too many meetings. It is a vicious circle. Someone cannot attend a meeting because they have another meeting. The attendees want the absent person's input or ideas before making a decision or taking action so they schedule another meeting. Do not do it. If the absent person's input is critical, assign the decision maker or issue owner to speak with the person offline and then move forward with a decision or action.
- Do not produce minutes. Document decisions or actions with names and due dates.
- Reduce the frequency of meetings. Change biweekly meetings to once every three weeks. Can you change your monthly standing meetings to every five or six weeks?
- Color-code your calendar. This is a great way to determine, at a glance, how you are spending your time and where it is unbalanced. As an example, I use green for revenue-generating activities, blue for business development, yellow for self-development activities, and red for personal items and holidays. If I am feeling overloaded, a quick review will identify to me where I need to build in more capacity and where I am devoting most of my time. This is a highly effective technique.

## Productive and Creative

It is important to be productive. It is equally important to be creative. Here are some ways to foster your creativity.

- *One hour of thinking time.* No technology. I do not recall where I heard this idea, but my clients and I have found it to be worthwhile. Take a pad of paper or a notebook and a pen—no tablet, laptop, or cellphone. Find a quiet location—an empty boardroom, a park bench, ideally not a busy coffee shop. For one hour, write down whatever comes to mind—ideas, a to-do list, random thoughts. Or doodle and draw—this is great stimulation for the right brain. Sometimes my clients identify a specific problem or issue to solve and spend the hour considering how to approach it.

- *Sleep.* I have joked with my family over the years that I am really easy to get along with after ten hours of sleep. I do not often sleep that long but eight to nine hours is most common for me and when on a restful holiday with no alarm, I often sleep ten hours. Not everyone requires this much sleep. However, in spite of people proudly saying they feel great on four hours per night or that they feel terrific when the alarm goes off at 4 a.m., there is considerable research to belie those claims. Our brains do not optimally function without six to eight hours of sleep. It is analogous to preventative maintenance on our vehicles or our equipment; there is a cost when we forego sleep.
- *Holidays—take them.* Every year. Your full entitlement. If you are in the midst of an M&A, a crisis from a safety incident, I will give you a let. However, you and I both know that is the exception not the norm. You need time away from work to regain and retain perspective and objectivity. You will be a better leader as a result. Your team members will benefit from solving issues independent of you and their relationships may improve as a result.

## Coaching and Mentoring

As a leader you are both a coach and a mentor. These terms are often used synonymously but they are different and each is uniquely powerful.

### Coaching

When coaching, ask questions and provide specific targeted feedback.

Questioning

You: "The product sales have declined in the northwest region YOY. What is contributing to this?"

Direct report or employee at lower level in the company: "The economy has hurt our clients in that region as they are heavily reliant on tourism and people are staying home."

You: "What actions have you taken in the past, in other regions to successfully remedy this?"

Specific and Targeted Feedback

You: "Last month you identified two actions to address declining product sales in the NW. I am glad to see you attended client meetings with our three biggest customers in that region. You also committed to asking each of the general managers for an action plan. I understand you did not receive plans from George and Leslie.

When you do not hold them accountable, it sends an unintended message to everyone—that you are not holding everyone to the same high standard and that there are no consequences to not following through on their commitments. As you know, I do hold each of you to account. When will you have action plans from George and Leslie so that you and I can review them?"

When coaching, you hold people to account. Wherever possible, your feedback should be on the basis of data and/or observed behavior. The coachee commits to actions with dates and your role is to follow up and ensure that the coachee follows through.

## *Mentoring*

Mentoring is a reactive activity. When you are mentoring a direct report or a high potential individual, you make yourself available to respond to questions; act as a trusted confidante; listen and guide. When mentoring, you are not holding someone to account, you are there to listen and provide resources such as books or introductions to others who could help and to share your experiences.

Ideally some of your interactions with your direct reports take the form of mentoring. Unless you are addressing performance gaps and/or substandard results against plan, mentoring can be highly effective. When mentoring, you can share mistakes you made and what you learned, you can validate what they are already thinking or doing as, often times, they are on the right track. When mentoring you need not ask for commitment to action or set a date for follow up. It can be a highly empowering exercise for the person you are speaking with and rewarding for you.

## Leading in Difficult Times: Growth through Pain

It is a sometimes-painful irony of life that we may learn the most about ourselves when life throws us a curve ball. So it is with the leadership. We fully discover our strengths and shortcomings when we are tested by adversity. How we deal with it and what we learn is central to who we are and our credibility as leaders. In bad times, all eyes are on the leader. How you behave has a tremendous impact on your people.

There are many factors that contribute to stretching your leadership abilities. Many of these will be familiar to you: economic lassitude, changes in foreign exchange, disappointing financial returns and associated cost pressures, declining sales, competitive pressures, conflict among team members, or a deteriorating relationship with your boss, colleagues or members of your team are but a few of the contributors. Across industries and geographies, when people are under stress for sustained periods of time, there are predictable outcomes. Fortunately, there are also practical leadership approaches to mitigate the risks to your business.

Many of your staff will become increasingly wary and tend to interpret each new sign as an indication of more bad things to come. Negative emotions run high and people are more likely to experience conflict and openly display frustration. They may become skeptical of the new or different and prone to reject it out of hand. As the stress continues, fatigue sets in and they become pessimistic about the future. Relationships can suffer as the focus becomes increasingly work-related.

> Walter Kresic, the Vice President of Pipeline Integrity for Enbridge. His company transports an average of 2.5 million barrels of crude oil across North America every day. Enbridge prides themselves on operating the longest and arguably the most sophisticated oil and liquids transportation system on the planet. Walter's job is to ensure that the

pipelines are well maintained, safe, and reliable. He oversees "a very large and complex program" with an annual budget of close to $1 billion. He knows that communities spanning the continent are reliant on him, his teams and staff on the ground to "not spill a drop."

When forest fires raged in northern Canada or when there have been are threats to pipeline safety, it can be a very stressful environment. Walter's colleagues cite him as someone who stays very calm under pressure. I asked him how he achieves this as in high-risk situations, Walter may be asked to update the board, communicate to a variety of stakeholders including politicians, aboriginal leaders, landowners, and employees.

The stress is real and "others are not seeing the stress that happens off line. The stress results from a compelling aim to understand the problem so that when advice and direction has to be provided, it can be provided with confidence." Walter quickly evaluates options and determines "an endgame." "The stress and the fuss happen off line so then when [I] have to create alignment, I have the background and the knowledge to present the goal. Everything goes smoothly when you have a plan (with basis behind it). It may look smooth on the outside, but it is a mission critical exercise on the inside."

We discussed the fact that highly effective executives understand that their role is often performing triage. "Triage is a system. You do not have to reinvent the wheel. Get to know the system and use it." I agree with him. When you operate from this perspective, you will rely on better judgment, act with consistency and predictability and mitigate risk.

His advice for dealing with a crisis or turbulent operating environment is, "at any given moment in time, whether you have all the information you would like or not, you have to be ready to make a decision. e.g., we need this important piece of information but we will proceed and come back to this late, making an adjustment if required". As an engineer, he spoke of the transition that technical experts must make to be highly effective leaders, particularly in turbulent times.

"The trick is that when you go from your training to a business situation, the pressure is real. If you don't know, don't fake it." Approach

(*Continued*)

it from a design perspective as you have been trained and consider "how are you going to deal with [this] situation?"

Not all highly intelligent, technical people can make this transition. When asked, "how do you develop this capability in your direct reports?" He responded "through mentorship and allowing for failure." Walter benefited from both of these. His advice is to "come clean and admit the mistake. Then continue to hone your skills so that you can make these decisions more quickly. [With experience] you can combine [knowledge from your past] decisions and make a decision more rapidly." After being in many crises situations, "one part of his brain has been exercised that way a lot."

## Keys to Leadership Success

Decades of research describe three elements of effective management in stressful times: task, people, and self-management.

- *Task management* is the leader's ability to set goals, organize efforts, direct activity, provide corrective feedback, and set the general focus of efforts.
- *People management* identifies the importance of communication, motivation, and encouragement. The ability to set the emotional tone of the workplace and inspire greater effort from others is the hallmark of a transformational leader. Operating in a stressful environment actually tends to increase the leaders' impact. People look at leaders more in hard times, partly as a product of the ambiguity that adversity creates.
- *Self-management* includes managing your behavior in ways conducive to more positive morale and action from your people, and helping them manage their own attitudes and behaviors toward appropriate outcomes.

The best leaders focus on all both task and people management in times of stress.

*Task Management*

From a task standpoint, the critical challenge is keeping people focused on things that are under their control. You may not be able to affect what happens in the stock market, but you can reach out to your customers and provide great service. This sense of control helps people manage their stress and allows them to experience small wins that have a buffering effect.

It is critical that leaders provide a broader vision of the future and a sense of direction and purpose. By linking today's actions to a better future, people gain a sense of perspective. Pointing out how one's individual job links to a broader corporate strategy, provides a sense of purpose and utility. A sense of purpose can provide significant relief from the debilitating effects of stress. Although many people draw their sense of purpose from broader life activities, a business leader can help provide the same sense at work.

*People Management*

On the people side, the key task of a leader is regular, honest, candid, and consistent communication. The leader must be seen as a reliable source of information, even when it means admitting you do not know. Equally important is listening. By understanding people's concerns, leaders can more readily address them and share with them the information and insights that will help reduce misunderstandings and deplete negative rumors.

In tough times, it is critically important to find opportunities for positive emotion. While a sense of humor helps, it is also important to celebrate wins, find ways to have fun, and thank people. Emphasizing strengths, wins, and good news helps redirect people's attention. While few people would wish to go through a difficult personal or professional challenge again, most recognize the benefits.

Seeing current circumstances as contributing to our resilience helps to make us more resilient.

*Self-management*

Self-management includes managing your behavior in ways conducive to more positive morale and action from your people, and helping them manage their own attitudes and behaviors toward appropriate outcomes. It is natural for people to feel powerless and victimized in tough times, so it is important for the leader to help his or her people shift from the mindset of the passive victim observing things from the sidelines to that of the athlete playing the game. Anything you can do to keep them focused on the fact that we always have choices and that, although we may not always control the final score, we do control how we play. If we play with integrity, stamina, optimism, and intensity, we can often surprise ourselves. Even if we fall short of our expectations, we can be proud of our performance.

It starts with a look in the mirror. You are the role model. You set the tone. If you are positive, confident, and optimistic, your people are likely to behave the same way. If you display focus and determination, they are likely to follow suit. Remember, just as panic and despair are infectious, so are energy and enthusiasm. In the words of Gandhi: "be the change you want to see in the world."

Multifaceted leadership is like the colors of light through a prism. To be most effective, you alter your leadership style for differing situations and people and in response to changing external and internal factors. Throughout every situation there is a thread of accountability—you demonstrate integrity as you do what you said you would do and you consistently hold others to account. Multifaceted leaders understand the imperative to nurture creativity while fostering productivity—in themselves and others.

# CHAPTER 6

# Harnessing Performance

Too many organizations are experiencing the opportunity costs of employee disengagement and underperformance. Often leaders do not understand how to unleash the untapped passion and capabilities of their teams. This chapter will provide you with inspiring, practical, and executable models and methods to overcome the employee lassitude that spans the globe and reinvigorate the workforce.

While greater than two-thirds of employees can be considered disengaged, there are two mechanisms that can effectively increase engagement, employee productivity, and retention within several months. These are alignment and clarity.

## Generating Power through Alignment

The majority of employees want meaning in their work. They want to make a contribution they can be proud of. They are not working for the compensation (although insufficient and inequitable compensation is a detractor, higher levels of compensation do not correlate to higher levels of satisfaction or "happiness").

When you link department, division, and individual goals and key performance indicators (KPIs) to the company's most important goals—what the president and CEO is speaking about publicly and internally, what customers have said is important, and what makes a difference in the communities in which they live and work—then you have alignment. It is powerful in its simplicity. Do not underestimate it.

An excellent example of this is a large bank that consistently, year-over-year, creates a plumb line of alignment from the CEO to those on the front line.

For the purposes of illustration, we will demonstrate how one of the performance goals for the fiscal year is cascaded throughout the organization (Figure 6.1).

By breaking targets down to a daily metric, employees have a greater line of sight to their performance. They are better equipped to achieve their goals, as they can adjust their actions more rapidly. Strong performers are motivated when they see their results tracking ahead of plan. This also gives managers and executives the data they need to more proactively track and manage performance.

When the goals of any and every employee can be tracked backup through the organization to the company's strategy and stated priorities, you create a powerful momentum of alignment. Like a team of horses harnessed together, the collective energy is greater than the sum of its parts.

In addition, most people, even the most ambitious and goal-driven individuals, are energized when they are contributing to a larger enterprise as part of a team. By linking every objective to departmental, regional, divisional, and/or corporate objectives, everyone sees how their role contributes to the whole. They are also more likely to highlight and

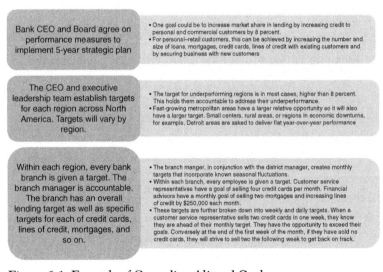

Figure 6.1 *Example of Cascading Aligned Goals*

express frustration with individuals or departments that are not pulling their weight. This is healthy and productive. It can create discomfort for leaders who are not holding themselves or their teams to account—as it should.

Establishing goal alignment as described above is a great start. About one-half of organizations have this level of goal setting. What differentiates an accountable organization that holds everyone's feet to the fire is how they consistently review the aligned goals:

- All results are published across the company as often as weekly and no less than once per month. There is complete transparency to everyone's results.
- The CEO reviews the aggregate results for company. Her direct reports review the regional results. Middle management leaders review the results by region and branch and, perhaps, by employee.
- The CEO reviews results with her leadership team as frequently as monthly for a midsized organization and quarterly for a Fortune 1000 organization.
- The executive team reviews results with their direct reports—vice presidents, assistant vice presidents, and/or district managers as frequently as once per week and no less than once per month.
- The branch managers review results with their staff at least weekly and often two or three times during a week. This frequency is particularly effective when the results are exceeding plan or falling below expectations.

## The Role of Reward and Recognition

Many of the organizations that conduct these practices also incorporate reward and recognition programs. Some utilize campaigns, contests, or celebrations. The most effective reward programs are not large-scale corporate events, but rather localized programs led by middle managers with attendance by executives. The reason for this is that employees most closely associate and identify with their immediate management.

In addition, most employees believe that they can achieve performance equal to that of their peers, but may feel that other regions or countries have advantages over their locale.

Sometimes friendly competition is highly effective. Both individual competitions and team competitions can be equally effective. When seeking to build team cohesiveness as well as generate results, creating competitions between offices, regions, or countries can be a great choice.

Remember the importance of simplicity. A phone call or e-mail from an executive acknowledging performance or extra effort during an important project goes a long way. A CEO told me about walking around the office to thank employees for their contribution and to wish them a happy holiday. It had been a particularly difficult year for the company and the industry. One employee said to her, "In my 30 years with the organization, the CEO has never come around to thank us." In fact, she had when she took on the role a few years earlier, but that is OK. This employee no doubt shared this with his family and friends his pleasant astonishment at the CEO's actions. Small actions can make a powerful impact.

When these actions are performed consistently, there is a cadence of accountability. This creates predictability and consistency. These are the hallmarks of integrity. The leaders do what they say they will do. They focus on and speak about what is most important.

In the next section, we will review the structure for goal setting and regular performance management. I will also outline the process for addressing substandard performance.

## The Mirror of Clarity

A culture of accountability benefits everyone—shareholders, customers, and employees (Figure 6.2). A cornerstone of creating this culture is clarity—clear expectations and transparent and specific feedback. These create a virtuous cycle. Do your direct reports understand explicitly what is expected of them? Have you discussed that their performance is measured both by quantitative measures and behavioral measures?

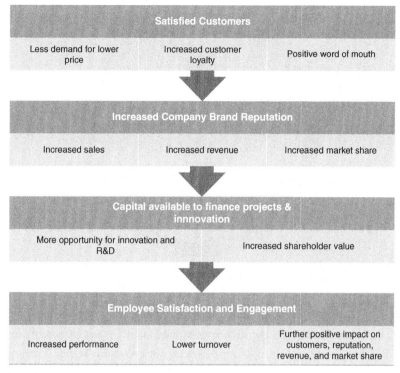

*Figure 6.2 Benefits of Managing to Performance*

## Factors for Success

The most meaningful discussions and resulting documents are created through shared accountability. The employee should prepare by completing each of the annual/midyear reviews and career-planning document in advance of the meeting. This is also the case for the monthly coaching meetings. When an employee arrives to the discussion without having adequately prepared, the best action is to reschedule the meeting. This clearly communicates the expectation of responsibility and holds them to account.

Ask each of your direct reports to echo back to you what they believe you are expecting them to deliver—both results and leadership behaviors. This will identify any hidden gaps in understanding and expectations. Are your direct reports clear on what results represent expected performance and what indicates exceptional performance? Avoid disappointment and surprises when assigning ratings and bonuses by discussing this when you are setting goals and at a midyear review.

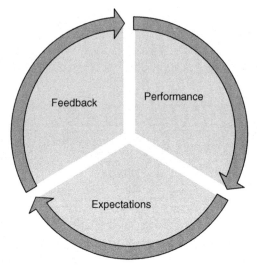

*Figure 6.3 Harnessing Performance*

A hallmark of accountable organizations is that the leaders and employees understand the difference between activity and results. Being very busy and completing a lot of tasks do not necessarily result in strong performance. Long hours at the office or working nights and weekends are also not directly correlated to performance.

Set targets. Measure results. Provide feedback. Recognize and reward. Repeat. Activity is largely irrelevant—except when it links directly to generating results for your most important priorities (Figure 6.3).

## Casting Out Poor Performance

What is the cost of substandard performance in your organization? Do you think you have an accurate estimate? What is included in that calculation? It can be easy to under-represent the total cost of substandard performance. Like a stone dropped into a still pond, the ripples can be widespread. Consider the following:

The great news is that you can intercept and positively impact this value chain early on or at any point along the way. Managing substandard performance is simple (Table 6.1). I expect you already know that. You mostly know how to do it or you would not be in the role you are in. It is uncomfortable and you may feel ill equipped. That is very

Table 6.1 Feet to Fire Performance Management Process

| | Outcome | Comments | Timing | Frequency |
|---|---|---|---|---|
| Annual Performance Setting | - Goals directly tied to corporate objectives<br>- 3–5 goals or KPIs<br>- 1–3 measures for each KPI | Measureable—dates to be completed; revenue $s to be obtained; budget to be met; FTE targets; sales goals, and so on. | Before end of first month of fiscal year | Annually |
| Coaching Meetings | - Review progress against most important goals<br>- Follow up on commitments from prior meeting<br>- Provide candid and specific feedback on performance<br>- Provide positive or developmental feedback on observed behaviors | - Frequency depends on level of individual. Executive reviews may be quarterly.<br>- May be conducted virtually over phone or Skype. | Throughout the year following goal setting at beginning of the year. | Weekly, biweekly, monthly, or quarterly |
| Midyear Review | - Review progress against goals<br>- Review progress against 3 KPIs and supporting objectives | - Discussion should reflect regular coaching sessions<br>- there should be no surprises particularly developmental feedback | Identify 1–3 actions<br>By end of month following middle of fiscal year | Annually |
| Career and Life Planning | - Set 2–3 development actions | - Each action should be tied directly to a development area, such as business acumen, team leadership, individual leadership, teamwork, and so on.<br>- As part of succession planning, this is often the opportunity to discuss mobility | - After completion of annual goal setting<br>- A separate meeting or discussion from the setting meeting | Once each year to discuss career interests, potential, capability, interests and once each year to review progress on actions and skill development |
| Performance Improvement Plan | - Identify and document specific functional or behavioral results that are not being met<br>- Confirm expectations and set targets and expectations | - Behavioral improvements required can include bullying or overly aggressive behavior, not taking accountability for performance of team or personal results, frequent absenteeism, consistently late arrival to meetings, use of profanity, and so on. | - When performance is not meeting expectations and improvement is not being achieved through regular coaching sessions and follow on actions | Biweekly for middle management and more junior. Monthly to quarterly for executive positions as it takes longer to impact broader and higher level goals. |

## Exercise 1 – Creating a plan for accountability

| Name: Shelley Miller | Position: Vice President Operations | Date: Oct 15 20XX |
|---|---|---|

| |
|---|
| **Company Vision:** Solutions for every home |
| Company Priorities for current year:<br>✓ Revenue growth<br>✓ Increase customer satisfaction<br>✓ Employee retention<br>or<br>**Single/primary focus for the year:** Growth; Integration; Expense Management; Client Focus |
| My Key Performance Indicators for the year:<br>• Operations meet or exceed all quality metrics and on-time delivery<br>• Customer Net Promoter score=>83%<br>• Improve employee engagement score by 3%<br>• Reduce operating, management and administrative expenses by 10% YOY |
| Three achievements in last 30/60/90 days<br>•<br>•<br>• |
| Other notable achievements<br>•<br>• |
| Internal or external factors are or may impact my ability to achieve results<br>•<br>• |
| Actions being taken to address these risks. |
| What I require from others, if anything. |
| Commitments for next 30/60/90 days<br>•<br>•<br>• |

common. The good news is that you can become more effective at addressing poor performance and, when you do so early and consistently, everyone wins—your customers, all employees, you, and the shareholders. Let us define the steps here.

## Turning Poor Performance on Its Head

### Individual

Behavioral Gaps

- Increased absenteeism
- Altered communication style—more abrupt, less responsive, defensive, sharing less information, displays of anger or frustration
- Not holding direct reports accountable and potentially making excuses
- Not meeting commitments
- Requiring follow-up to complete commitments
- Demonstrates poor judgment in decision making or interactions with others within or outside of work

Functional Performance Gaps

- Not reporting or under-representing errors, emissions, or incidents that could create material risk for the company
- Not actively contributing to business discussions or decisions
- Peers do not seek their expertise for their area of responsibility
- You are not satisfied with their displayed judgment for decisions or actions
- They do not demonstrate the appropriate level of urgency or severity when there are issues within their team and/or their area of responsibility
- You are uncomfortable delegating authority to them

### Performance of Team

- The department, division, or team is not meeting service level agreements or delivering on KPIs. Examples of this include:

sales team falling short on sales; marketing not meeting a deadline for new product launch; operations not meeting product quality or on time delivery; IS not meeting service level agreements or experiencing cyber-security breaches; governance team not delivering new policies on time in response to new regulatory requirements; or HR not completing board reporting in a manner the board expects.
- Not holding direct reports accountable and potentially even making excuses for them like "the customer changed their mind 3 times" or "the sales team make unrealistic promises."
- Not addressing underperforming employees. Similar to the above, this could be exhibited by the leader not addressing individual performance gaps through conversations and disciplinary action up to, and including, termination.

### *Knowledge or Acumen*

1. Your power lies in establishing clear performance expectations upfront. If you have not set, communicated, and documented the KPIs for the year, do that first.
2. Establish regular one-on-one meetings—face-to-face or virtually and at a realistic frequency. For executive roles, this may be once per month; for those newer in role or to the organization/industry, or more junior in the organization, this may be biweekly. What is important is that you make these meetings a priority. Few of us have any, let alone lots of, extra capacity in our workdays. There may often be competing priorities. Providing leadership and direction to your team members is one of your KPIs. If, once these are in place, the performance is not meeting your expectations; it is appropriate to adjust your approach.
3. Start with a candid conversation. This is often the hardest part and thus where we delay or figuratively drag our feet. This can lead to growing frustration for both of you. When people are not meeting our expectations, they often sense that based on our interactions and/or they intuitively know they are not contributing commensurate with their capability.

Situation: Discussing Poor Performance

Before you have the conversation, consider: is this level of performance unusual for this person? Have they previously been reliable or a good performer? If this is a change in performance and particularly if it is a change in behavior, there may be external factors at play that you are not aware of. These could include relationship issues with a spouse, child or other close family member, health issues for the individual or someone close to them, financial issues, and so on. If they have previously been a strong performer, ensure that you first seek information from them to determine if there are any external factors or extenuating circumstances.

Are they in a new role or new to the industry? Could this altered performance be grounded in a lack of confidence, or a steep learning curve?

Ask questions. First seek their input. Frame it as a request for their feedback and using language that is natural for you,

"Thank you for meeting today. I would like to discuss the performance of your department or division" or "I would like to hear your thoughts on your performance so far this year/quarter."

*If the individual discloses an external issue,* (e.g., medical, family), you will want to offer confidentiality and whatever assistance you can such as pointing them to employee assistance program if you have one. Ideally, ask them what you can do to help. They may say no assistance is required. Do not take on their problems, but discuss accommodations that may be required and for how long and how you will work together. In some cases, a health leave may be required and you will need to find an interim successor. Or they may require flexibility to attend medical appointments with family member.

It is important to clearly define your expectations of their performance while offering support.

If there are no external or mitigating issues and you *attribute the performance gap to a learning curve* (e.g., first executive appointment or new industry), be prepared to offer suggestions of how they can bolster their performance.

Successful strategies in this scenario can include attendance at conferences, joining an industry association, or formal executive development through an accredited college or university.

When performance does not improve or the employee does not demonstrate commitment to change their practices, a more formal process is required. This is when you really need to hold their feet to the fire.

- Schedule biweekly or monthly meetings (no less than monthly)
- Document specific KPIs and performance metrics
- Document actions to be taken by employee
- Review at each meeting
- Document

## Exercise 2– Recording and reporting progress (template)

The following template is very effective for recording and reporting on measures and progress. It also provides the audit trail you may require should you enter in any legal disputes in future.

| Performance Goal | Metrics | Action | Due Date | Completed Y/N (if Y—as per expectations?) |
|---|---|---|---|---|
| Build stronger relationships with direct reports | No reported incidents from employees | Meet with each employee one-on-one and ask for feedback | By April 30 | |
| | Increase employee engagement scores from 65% to 70% by year end | Participate in 360-degree review with external coach | By May 15 | |
| | | Debrief with me and identify one action | By May 30 | |
| Increase your integrity by meeting commitments | No follow-up required by me | | Immediately | |
| | No reported incidents of missed reporting to CFO, HR or others | | Every month end and quarter end | |

Manager_____ Employee_____ Date_____

## Powerful Feedback

Whether providing feedback at a monthly coaching session after observing strong performance or during a midyear review, how you provide the feedback can have a big impact on future results.

- Be consistent—provide feedback with examples at every coaching session.
- Be specific—"in the meeting with our executive team today, you listened without interrupting. This is a great improvement as at prior meetings, as we have discussed, you interrupted people frequently, particularly those who speak slowly."
- Be timely—feedback holds the most power when it closely follows the observed behavior or results (e.g., sales team exceeded forecast for the second quarter in a row).
- Be bold—do not hold back because you are uncomfortable with conflict. If you anticipate an emotional reaction, prepare in advance with a trusted colleague or with HR. Also, if your employee has reacted negatively in the past, consider why this may be happening so that you can better prepare with questions.
- Be selective—if you have not observed an issue but have heard about it from others, ask them to address the issue.
- Ask questions—"This product launch was the most successful we have had in two years. What specifically did your team do differently or in advance of the launch that contributed to this success?"
- Leave the meeting with nothing left unsaid—after you have completed a coaching session, ask yourself, "is there anything I did not say?" If so, ask yourself why you held back. You will know you are having highly effective meetings when you leave with nothing left unsaid.

## Summary

By creating alignment and providing clarity for your team or your company, you can harness the collective intellect and creativity of your employees. Most people want to make a meaningful contribution in their work. Next, your role is to recognize and reward the right behaviors and address underperformance without hesitation. With increased engagement come higher levels of performance. Higher levels of individual and team performance maximize profitability and everyone benefits.

## Blank accountability plan (Exercise 1)

| Name: | Position: | Date: |
|---|---|---|
| Company Vision: | | |
| Company Priorities for current year: <br> ✓ <br> ✓ <br> ✓ <br> OR <br> Single/primary focus for the year: | | |
| My Key Performance Indicators for the year: <br> • <br> • <br> • <br> • | | |
| Three achievements in last 30/60/90 days <br> • <br> • <br> • | | |
| Other notable achievements <br> • <br> • | | |
| Internal or external factors are or may impact my ability to achieve results <br> • <br> • | | |
| Actions being taken to address these risks. | | |
| What I require from others, if anything. | | |
| Commitments for next 30/60/90 days <br> • <br> • <br> • | | |

# CHAPTER 7

# Talent for the Twenty-First Century

High-performing organizations consider talent management a strategic priority, equal to that of financial performance and other imperatives. Unlike organizations with lackluster performance, high-achieving organizations take a long-term view of talent management, governing results and adjusting structures as required. This chapter provides the compelling evidence for a robust talent management practice. The chapter equips leaders with the tools and practices to become world class, enabling heightened corporate performance.

## Overcoming the Succession Crisis

Succession planning is an increasingly important priority for many executive teams and their boards. I have evidenced an emerging crisis for the past several years.

### Few Immediate and Ready Successors

When asked, CEOs of mid- and large-sized firms, and their boards, can identify successors who will be ready for the top job in five to ten years. Few of them can identify strong and viable successors who are ready immediately or anticipated to be ready in the next one to three years.

One does not have to search far to identify examples.

> When Valeant Pharmaceuticals CEO Michael Pearson took medical leave in late 2015, his vacancy was filled by creating two committees—the first comprised of an executive vice president and general counsel,

*(continued)*

an executive vice president and company group chairman and an independent director and the second committee to oversee the interim directorial committee comprised of an independent director, president ValueAct Capital and the former CFO for Valeant.

In addition to the at worst, ineffective nature of committees and at best, the dysfunction created when there are competing agendas, egos and no clearly identified leader, Pearson's absence occurred at a difficult time for Valeant. Investors were already skittish following an accounting scandal and a fifty-percent decline in share price in a few short months. Those circumstances are analogous to the anxiety following attacks such as the Paris bombings or the 2013 Boston Marathon bombing. The community looks to the most senior leader and his or her behavior and from there, they take their lead on how severely to interpret the situation and what action they should take.

In 2012, Hal Kvisle, corporate director and former CEO of TransCanada, was asked by the Talisman Energy board to step out of retirement to replace John as CEO. Originally rumored to be a six-month assignment, Mr. Kvisle's stated objectives were to revamp the company, its strategy and expenses and assist with the placement of a new CEO. His tenure as Talisman CEO lasted until early 2015 when Talisman was sold to Repsol.

## *Demographics*

There has been so much commentary about baby boomers, millennials, generation Xs and Ys that some lassitude has set in. Whether you believe the generations are largely similar or vastly different, the fact remains that the retirements and changing priorities of boomers will result in a number of vacant senior leadership positions. The other result these demographics play is that many organizations of $10M to $500M will be available for sale in the near future as founders seek to fund their next phase of life.

Many presidents and CEOs have had their heads down for years running their businesses. As they lift their heads and start to plan for retirement in one to three years, they realize that there are few, if any, on their executive leadership team that will be ready for the top job as quickly as ideal.

## Changing Face of Retirement

Although retirements among the relatively large boomer population will create vacancies, it will not be in a straightforward manner. Many retirees want to maintain the intellectual stimulation they received in the workplace. Most also want the freedom to travel to escape cold winters or oppressively hot and humid summers, dedicate more time to volunteer activities, spend time with family, focus on health and wellness, and pursue new or abandoned hobbies.

This combination of interests is a boon to receptive organizations. Highly skilled technicians or those with specialized knowledge, such as expertise in mergers and acquisitions or regulatory compliance, may be interested in mentoring others, consulting, or contributing to complex projects on a part-time basis—for a defined duration or part of each week, part of each month, from a remote location, and so on. Utilizing capable professionals in this manner is a win–win. Expenses are reduced and you have access to specialized skills from individuals who have a proven track record and know how to get things done.

Some of the successful models include:

- Working nine to ten months per year for the final three to five years of employment, retaining health benefits but no pay during the absence.
- Consulting post retirement for a specific project or length of time or on retainer. A fixed fee will benefit both parties. As a company, you have cost certainty and will not find yourself held hostage to hourly billing should the consultant or contractor not deliver as expected. This can include mentoring to transition a new executive, specialized advice on a particular project, and so on.
- Consulting or advice provided virtually. Much knowledge work does not require face-to-face or hands-on interaction. Seize the advantages of Skype and other services. You can avoid some or all travel costs and if the consultant lives or is vacationing in another country (e.g., Canada or the United States). You may also be able to pay in their local currency and benefit from foreign exchange rates.

## Creating Robust Talent Management and Succession Planning Practices

Companies face big challenges when they lack appropriate talent management and succession planning. While an effective process requires discipline, it need not be onerous or time-consuming. The plan can be scalable.

While demographics will lead to increased vacancies across sectors, it will be felt particularly acutely in roles with specialized knowledge, those with

*Table 7.1 Performance Management Framework*

| Actions conducted with employees | Frequency | By whom |
|---|---|---|
| Identify career interests, goals, capabilities, mobility, long-term aspirations | Annually | Employee prepares and provides to leader for discussion at career planning and development discussion |
| Share information about how the leadership team views the employee. Refer to 360-degree reviews or other data-based information. Identify strengths and development areas, functional and/or behavioral. Share how the organization views the employee's potential. Discuss potential next job and longer term roles. | Annually | Leader |
| Discuss methods and ways of further leveraging strengths and ways to fill gaps in knowledge or experience. | | |
| Create development plan for review with immediate leader | Annually | All employees in leadership roles All employees in key roles (e.g., specialized, highly technical or unique and one-off position) |
| Employee and leader discuss, confirm funding if appropriate and sign-off | Annually | Every leader with his or her direct reports |
| Review progress against development objectives and achievement of committed actions, (e.g., external executive leadership training, MBA, participation on specific project or initiative, executive coaching, technical training, association membership, and so on). | Mid-year | Every leader with his or her direct reports |

many years of experience, and senior leadership roles. For specialized and technical roles in engineering, aerospace, and large infrastructure/capital projects, judgment, problem solving and risk assessment capabilities follow years of practical experience in addition to technical training and education. Consider a board of directors for a large publicly or privately held company—advanced degrees and/or professional accreditation such as a CFA will be beneficial to management, but cannot be substituted for years of management experience and the wisdom acquired from successes and failures.

Well-executed succession planning considers roles with specialized knowledge and skill as well as leadership roles and includes both categories in its talent management practices (Table 7.1).

## Talent Management and Succession Planning Process (Table 7.2)

*Assess potential:*

- *Well placed:* remain in current role for next one to three years. Assess in future.
- *Medium potential:* has potential for role one level higher.
- *High potential:* has potential for a role two or more levels higher in the company.

*Note performance rating (from most recent annual review):*

- *Developing*—for those new to role
- *Meets*—for those consistently meeting performance expectations and KPIs
- *Exceeds*—for those consistently exceeding expectations
- *Needs improvement*—an employee who is no longer consistently meeting objectives or was previously developing but should be fully performing by this time

Some organizations choose to have one more rating between meets and exceeds.

*Timeframe:*

- Ready now
- one to two years
- two to three years

Table 7.2 Talent Management & Succession Planning Framework

| Name | Current role | Assessed Potential | Timing | Development plans | Potential roles | Performance rating | Mobility |
|---|---|---|---|---|---|---|---|
| John Carter | Vice President Supply Chain | Well placed | 2–3 years | Attend Supply Chain conference in Nevada in June | N/A | Meets | N/A |
| Teresa Jones | CIO | Medium potential | 1 year | Harvard or Stanford Executive development program in fall Participate in launch of new product offering in China | SVP Marketing, SVP Pacific region | Exceeds | 1 |
| Frank Linkletter | Director, Product | High potential | 2–3 years | | VP Sales, SVP Marketing | Exceeds | |

*Mobility\*:*

- Local (L)—within forty-five to sixty miles of current geographic area
- Regional (R)
- National (N)
- International (I)

A simple and straightforward process for review of succession plans is as follows:

1. Every leader completes a succession assessment for his or her direct reports, as per the example above.
2. At an executive meeting once each year, every senior leader or executive shares the information for his or her department or division. Include your most senior HR person.
3. Little discussion is required for those who are well placed. In future years, they may be denoted as high potential in which case the group may want to have more discussion.
4. Each leader presents the rationale for those identified as *medium or high potential,* particularly for those who are identified as having high potential. The leader also identifies the proposed actions for development. This is useful as other leaders can offer their shared experience or ideas for development.
5. It is also important to identify those who are not meeting expectations and the action plans expected to remediate the performance gaps. This contributes to a culture of accountability. The leader shares responsibility with the employee to improve performance. If a leader identifies an employee as *needs improvement* for two cycles (e.g., over two years or two successive talent management meetings) the presenting leader should be held accountable to proceed with termination or a job change for the incumbent.

### Important Considerations

To ensure your talent management process contributes to the desired end state—succession for the organization, particularly for executive and key

---

*This may or may not be applicable or required for your company

roles—*it is important to gain consensus and agreement for medium and high potential candidates. This addresses variations in performance and potential measures and standards within organizations. As a rule of thumb, if other executives in the company do not broadly know an employee, that employee cannot be assessed as high potential.*

Senior leaders are regularly called upon to influence and collaborate with their peers and colleagues inside and outside of the company. Their peer relationships are as important as relationships with their direct reports. For C-suite executives, external relationships carry even greater weight of importance. If a leader is strongly supportive of an employee and believes they have the potential for the most senior roles in the company but that person is not broadly known, a primary development goal should be increased exposure. Actions to achieve this can include assignment to projects, an assigned executive mentor, or inclusion in executive meetings.

In a large organization, an executive may have the overall responsibility for hundreds of people. In these situations, the most effective practice is for the vice presidents and directors, or equivalent, to conduct the process as outlined above. Then the CEO, COO, and others can participate in a meeting with VPs and above to review the already vetted list of high potentials.

### Development through Stretch Roles

A highly effective development activity can be putting someone into a stretch role. This can be accomplished by placing a long time operations leader into a marketing role, asking them to lead the Information Services group, or moving them to a leadership role in an unfamiliar market. It may take them well outside of their comfort zone and their area of expertise. The resulting benefits are that they will need to lean on others—internal and external colleagues and their staff—to further their functional knowledge. This can provide the space for direct reports to expand their responsibilities and scope while further developing the leader in his or her new role.

It affords the organization an opportunity to assess the leader's behavior in a stressful situation. It also broadens the leader's expertise, which enables him or her to make more informed decisions and a more meaningful contribution. Sometimes, the reporting executive would have preferred a different or known candidate and may undermine the candidate in the stretch role.

It is important that the individual's immediate leader and ideally the president or CEO actively sponsor and support this opportunity. It should be recognized that the incumbent may not perform at an exceptionally high level in this role, but that is not the goal; the goal is for them to be stretched and gently tested.

### Consistency Will Bear Fruit

A consistently applied talent management and succession planning process will pay massive dividends to your company over time. I have seen situations in which companies have discarded these practices during economic downturns. Talent management can become a lesser priority as there may be a greater supply of talented people in the market and retention may be less of a concern as employees stay with the devil they know versus the devil they do not know.

There are risks in dropping this strategic activity.

- Even in a downturn, and sometimes especially in a downturn, there are appealing opportunities available for top performers as companies weed out lesser performers and uplift their overall bench strength. You may lose your best people to your competitors.
- When the market improves, your talented employees will, as always, be the most marketable. You may also lose executives and senior leaders who delayed retirement or job moves because of the economy. As a result, you can emerge from a downturn and discover (a) you have fewer available successors for top roles and (b) the successors are three to four years away from being ready as you deferred developmental activities.
- Finally, when you turn on and off your talent management activities, you inadvertently send the messages that you do not hold yourselves accountable for sustaining strategic priorities and that ambitious employees may not have the career possibilities they are seeking.

## Carefully Managing Expectations

As we described earlier in this chapter, potential is distinct from performance. Performance measures result over a period of time, against specific goals and metrics. Career potential is a measure of one's believed future capability. The latter is assessed in part through demonstrated performance but also through considering emotional intelligence, executive presence, leadership behaviors, judgment, and decision-making.

When you advise someone that they have been identified as high potential, it is important to structure those first and subsequent conversations carefully. You want to identify to the employee that they are highly valued and that the organization considers them capable of taking on more senior roles. You want to encourage them to remain with the organization, as they will be given the opportunity to grow and develop and perhaps meet their personal and professional goals. You also need to advise them that there are no guarantees beyond your commitment to regularly and transparently speak with them about their development and potential.

I recommend encouraging them to keep the information confidential, as it can demotivate others who have not been identified as high potential. For C-suite roles, others can typically identify who are the heir apparents. If you are a publicly held company, you may wish to identify the one to three potential successors for the President and COO roles. Beware, when doing so, if you have not had well thought out conversations in advance with the executive team, or if this level of transparency is not consistent in your organization, I advise you wait until you create that culture, if ever, before disclosing such information.

An assessment of high potential does *not* mean:

- a promotion within any defined period of time
- a pay raise or higher bonus
- a guarantee of appointment to any particular role
- a high(er) performance rating

It should mean—a commitment from the immediate manager and the organization that you will assist them in further developing their skills and preparing them for future opportunities.

It is also important to remember that someone can remain high potential even when their performance is meeting but not consistently exceeding expectations. They may be in a stretch role, in a new and challenging role, or leading during an overly complex situation (e.g., post M&A integration, during a lawsuit, corporate crisis due to major safety incident, or a hostile takeover).

When an employee takes on a new role, particularly a stretch role, they may be evaluated as "well placed" when he or she was previously identified as being high potential. Potential is not static or limitless and will be evaluated by observing someone's capabilities in different roles.

Consistently high performance is not correlated directly to being identified as high potential. Someone may be a strong performer within their area of expertise but may not have the capability or the interest to take on greater responsibility or to work in a different domain.

These are the important characteristics to remember and share with all employees and particularly those who have been identified as high potential.

## Unleashing Your Racehorses

Some of your best performers may be your most insecure people. Part of their drive may stem from the belief that they regularly need to prove themselves and their capabilities—to themselves and others. This can benefit both of them and the company. (It does not typically cause an issue, unless they demonstrate bullying, poor listening skills, or other inappropriate behavior. If that is the case, refer to chapter six in which we outline how to deal with poor performance.) Top sales persons are a good example. In any industry, the top performing twenty percent of sales people typically contribute to eighty percent of the overall sales revenue. The offset to this can be that they readily move companies if they feel they are not being recognized or compensated appropriately for their contributions.

In the following, we will review how you best sustain the motivation and performance of your best performers without marginalizing the balance of your workforce.

Accept that aggregate employee performance follows a bell curve

- Five to ten percent of your employees, in any given year, will consistently exceed performance expectations, five to ten percent will perform below expectations, and most will meet or meet and sometimes exceed performance expectations. The performance ratings ascribed to employees should closely match this distribution—for the company overall and for each department and division.
- *If this is a new concept for your organization, you will likely receive some resistance, as managers believe that they have a particularly high number of high performers, or that none of their employees are performing below expectations.* This is particularly common when a department or team has successfully completed a challenging project or you have completed a major acquisition. In responding to this argument, it is important to remember that not everyone has equal opportunity in a given year to contribute well above expectations. A move to treat everyone as largely equal will create negative outcomes (i.e., rating twenty-five to thirty percent in the highest range or rating almost everyone as meeting expectations). You will demotivate and disincent your best performers.

Tenure is not directly correlated to performance

- Managers may argue that most of their employees have been with the company or in the industry for several years and equate that to a high-performance rating. This is particularly common in technical fields such as engineering, health care, and aerospace. In fact, there is often little correlation. You may observe complacency among long-term employees and new employees may introduce highly innovative or productive solutions.

Level of activity is rarely correlated with performance

- "I have been really busy this year." "I regularly put in 60-hour workweeks!" Most of us are familiar with the concept of the point of diminishing returns. This applies to working long hours. At some point, fatigue and absorption in work activities stifle creativity and sap productivity. When I was a corporate executive, some of my best people utilized their allotted vacation and worked a standard workweek most of the time. In fact, for other than senior executive roles, if someone cannot complete their priority objectives in a standard workweek, I can usually show them where they are inefficient and the opportunity costs.

The opportunity to excel may not be equal

- This can be difficult to communicate and for people to accept; however, it is a reality particularly in large organizations. Someone may be asked to contribute to a strategic initiative. External market conditions (i.e., demise of a competitor or surge in economic activity) may provide the opportunity to rapidly gain market share and surpass revenue targets. In these situations, those who leveraged these opportunities to deliver higher performance should be rewarded with a higher rating. Others may have envy the opportunities but may not have had the same opportunity and will receive a rating recognizing their satisfactory performance in a given year.

Link compensation directly to performance rating

- To incent and retain your highest performers and to maintain credibility put your money where your mouth is. Tie compensation directly to performance. Allocate a meaningful percentage of your overall budget to the top performers. Where performance did not meet expectations, there should be no merit increase. *This may not be possible when you have a collective agreement. This also does not apply to those who are new in role and developing.* If their performance has been as expected, a merit increase is appropriate. Without this, how will you motivate employees to pursue developmental roles?

## Special Circumstances

If your company has completed a large acquisition, an ERP project, or experienced any other widely impactful project or situation, there is another effective way to recognize everyone's contribution without undermining the performance distribution utilized above. In these situations, assign performance ratings as described earlier. In addition, provide a one-time payment to every contributing employee. This may encompass every employee in the company or those in a single division or department. The special payment can be an equal dollar amount for every employee or a fixed percentage of his or her base pay. You will determine the best choice for you based on the available and approved funding and the nature of the special project (e.g., corporatewide son or departmentwide).

Every organization will benefit from a robust talent management and succession planning process. It need not be arduous and the practices described in this chapter have been successfully utilized in $10 million and $3 billion companies as well as not for profits.

CHAPTER 8

# Elevating Others to Soar

## Leading Organizational Change

Most mergers and acquisitions fail to deliver the expected return on investment. Large capital projects and new systems do not always deliver promised productivity improvements or a better user experience. In spite of this, companies continue to launch new change efforts expecting different outcomes. Regardless of industry, organizations and governments cannot abandon their pursuit of excellence through change; to do so would stall progress. Given these challenges, the ability to effectively execute change will be a lasting and key differentiator.

We have tried change management and it does not work. Weary executives have collectively committed millions of dollars to change management programs, tools, workshops, and employee certification. The result has been a resoundingly hollow thud. In most organizations, adoption of new Enterprise Resource Planning (ERP) systems, desired cultural changes, or improved processes in operations, production, or accounting is slower than anticipated, wasting valuable resources. It does not have to be this way.

Given the challenges that accompany change, the ability to effectively execute change will always be a key way in which organizations are distinguished from each other. In spite of many years of continued change in North American organizations, seventy percent of these change efforts still fail to achieve the stated goals. Certainly, the pace of change varies somewhat by industry. Banking, telecommunications, and retail, for example, regularly launch new products and services, whereas utilities and energy companies, such as those in the oil and gas sectors, change at a much slower rate.

# Factors Influencing Change

*Internal and External*

Both internal and external factors can precipitate organizational change. Some notable recent events that externally catalyzed change include the tech bubble burst of 2000 and the global economic downturn in 2008. These economic factors affected many industries—banking, construction, real estate sales, retail sales, entertainment, and the food and beverage industry among them. Other than a troubled economy, external factors that may trigger change efforts are declining sales, increased commodity prices (as in the example above), and supplier or customer concerns.

> One particularly interesting case is how the market price of potash affected BHP Billiton, the world's largest mining company, which had considerable investments in Saskatchewan, Canada. It had recruited over six hundred people, relocating many from Australia, and had invested heavily in construction to develop the Jansen mine. In 2007, one ton of potash was nearly $1,000. By the summer of 2013, however, prices had dropped to $440 a ton. With this drop in potash prices, BHP moderated development, which resulted in changes to staffing levels and investment, although it did sustain the mining project.

Internal factors that become the impetus for organizational change include: declining employee morale, product quality issues, health and safety incidents, or increasing costs for employee compensation. Ironically perhaps, change is the only constant in business. Without it, there would be little or no progress, as businesses would stay safely within the familiar. Few failures, the result of few risks, limit opportunities for problem solving and learning, and the innovations that arise from these processes.

*Urgency*

The rate and pace of change varies by industry and organization, and often varies within a given industry or organization, depending on the pressure to respond to the internal or external catalysts. One further piece of this picture is the urgent need to address a sudden or pressing issue. Some examples are:

- avoiding job losses
- regaining lost market share
- avoiding bankruptcy
- avoiding a hostile takeover

At times like these, when change is urgently needed or a crisis is looming, leaders often intuitively recognize the need to be more decisive and will quickly move to action. Although they may be faced with difficult and emotionally charged options such as reducing staff, the best leaders make the tough decisions even in the face of heightened risk and urgency. What keeps them on track regardless of the difficult circumstances? They recognize their responsibility to all stakeholders—employees, customers, and shareholders.

### *Leading the Parade*

When you are the change sponsor, you may have initiated the project, the acquisition, or the replacement technology that is the central component of the change. As sponsor and/or champion, you understand the rationale for the change and the anticipated benefits. Successfully implementing the change is likely a key performance indicator and, therefore, may be linked to your compensation. You may have led a similar change at a different company or previously in your career. For all of these reasons, you likely have a level of tempered enthusiasm for the change. At minimum, you are armed with a much more comprehensive understanding of the change than most, if not all, other stakeholders internally and externally.

One of the most useful analogies to remember when you are leading a change effort is to envision yourself at the front of a parade. Let us use the Macy's Thanksgiving Day parade. The parade starts at Seventy-Seventh Street and Central Park West. Later it traverses along Central Park South. When it reaches Herald Square, it is approaching the termination point. For all the reasons noted in the paragraph above, when the change is launched, you have already experienced and likely come to terms with your own resistance, apprehension, and assessment of the risks of the change. In the parade analogy, you have already reached Central Park South. You have experienced the sights and sounds that others are only now encountering. While you are describing the flags out front of the Plaza and the horse-drawn coaches, others are still at Seventy-Seventh Street and Central Park West. Their scenery is completely different and they do not fully understand what you are describing. It does not match their view.

As the leader, you need to cast your thoughts back to the start of the parade and change. Did you wrestle with the practicality of the change? Were you concerned with the impact on customers and staff? Did you harbor doubts about achieving the ROI? You may feel frustrated because you are describing something that seems straightforward or because you feel you have delivered the message repeatedly. You may have. The fact that it is, for you to engage the hearts and minds of those responsible for making the change and/or to win over external detractors, you will have to explain and reinforce the key messages regularly. When you use the parade reference, it will help you understand and appreciate the way you need to describe *where you are on the route and what you see*. This creates a vision and direction for others. Use the parade to also *reflect on what you experienced and what questions you had* so that you can better respond to the resistance and questions from others.

In this section, we look at a model that will significantly step up your organization's ability to effectively lead change. Incorporating this model into your management approach will help you become a world-class change leader.

## THRIVE©: A Change Model for Leaders at Every Level

*Rationale* → *Roles* → *Behaviors* → *Monitor* → *Incorporate*

### 1. Rationale for change—identify and explain

Whatever the change in the works, some people within the company will view it favorably and others unfavorably. These varied perspectives result from changes they have experienced in the past and their level of trust in their manager and the leadership of the organization, among other factors. Mitigating resistance is much easier when people understand why the change is being made. Putting effort in at the front end of any change process will save a lot of time, frustration, and even more effort down the line. Consider how you can address this question: What is the rationale for a particular change?

Think about your own position as you begin to engage the change management. What was your role in how the change decisions were made? For instance, were you:

- the sponsor of the change?
- involved in the analysis?
- a participant in creating the business case?
- at the table when the decision was made?

To a greater or lesser degree, any of these roles place you in a privileged position compared to others in the organization. You have had time to think through the options, perhaps to explore alternatives. You may even have been the instigator of the change. This means that you have had time to consider personal implications of the change: Will it cause a loss or gain in your responsibilities? A loss or gain to your prestige or standing in the organization? In what other ways will the change affect the particulars of your situation? With this advance notice, your vantage point is much different than the person who is just now learning of the change, at a time when the process is already underway.

This is the essence of leading change. Being in on the change from the outset, you may have been involved in the planning and goal setting for weeks or months. Others, however, have not. Imagine placing yourself back at the beginning of the parade route where you have the opportunity to explain to others what is coming up. Provide them with a précis of the journey so far. Where appropriate, explain the analysis and considerations.

It is essential to explain the rationale for the decision and why it is important to the organization. If you miss this step and do not define why the change matters, before long you will discover that while you are moving forward in the change effort, others are not. When you turn around, your followers are lagging well behind, huddled together with looks of confusion, and asking questions that could have, and should have, been answered some time before.

Helping staff to understand the relevance or necessity of a change is *especially important* when change is urgent. This is when most employees look to their leaders for decisions, direction, and communication about the path ahead. Engaging employees in the sense of urgency requires that they understand the risks of not making the change. Staff, like leaders, will engage more quickly and with a deeper level of commitment when they appreciate the threat. It must clearly be visible so all understand that time is of the essence.

When there is no apparent urgency—as with many ongoing process improvement projects, office moves, or the introduction of a new business model—it is more difficult to implement the change at the expected pace. Therefore, when you are faced with a business problem that requires rapid resolution, be prepared to act decisively. Recognize the inherent value in an urgent problem, specifically that you will be able to more readily mobilize employee support for the change.

## 2. Roles and Responsibilities—Specify Early

In the midst of an organizational change, productivity can decline dramatically and quickly. This is particularly true in organizations that undergo change less often. Leaders and staff will be distracted, wondering how this change will affect them. Will it be favorable or unfavorable? However, the productivity drop is not inevitable and leaders' actions can mitigate this.

One important task is to identify leader and staff roles and accountabilities as early as possible. This provides people with certainty. Though some roles will remain as they were before the change, others will be significantly altered. Also, while some leaders will remain in their existing roles, others will not. Nonetheless, during the change execution process, everyone is still accountable to contribute appropriately to make the change successful.

An example that demonstrates how this may unfold is a large project focused on installing a new ERP system. This type of project is typically sponsored by the CIO and led by a senior program or project manager. During the initial stages of these initiatives, other business areas such as supply chain, human resources, sales, and operations may experience little impact to their day-to-day activities. Finance and accounting, however, are important contributors from the earliest stages of the project.

Implementing an ERP has wide-ranging impacts, as it will ultimately alter the work processes in most areas of a company. So, while the VP, Supply Chain, or Head of Sales and Marketing may feel they do not have a role to play, in fact, they do. They and all other leaders must positively represent the change to the employees in their area, and to their peers and colleagues. All leaders have a responsibility to listen for resistance and to proactively address it. They can best achieve this by reiterating the rationale for the change, as identified in Step 1.

*As a leader*, determine as early as possible:

- What decisions you will make independently?
- What decisions you will make following consultation with others?
- How you will delegate authority?
  - What decisions others will make?
  - Whom you will assign accountability to for various aspects of the implementation?

Once you have decided

- Review with those involved
- Communicate broadly to
  - direct reports
  - throughout the organization

When roles and accountabilities are not clearly understood

> "Janice" was the VP, Facilities, for Cyclone Sports when the company acquired a smaller retailer, a small competitor of a sporting goods company. Shortly thereafter, Cyclone decided to undertake a rebranding exercise. Prior to the acquisition, Janice had the centralized responsibility for all

*(continued)*

Cyclone retail stores and head office facilities. This included making all interior design decisions for all stores and offices. At Soccer Unlimited, this responsibility was decentralized. Therefore, Regional VPs sourced their own furniture and selected their preferred fixture suppliers.

The Cyclone Sports CEO was aware of the different operating models in the two organizations, but did not communicate to his executive leadership team that he had decided on the centralized model for the merged entity. Thus, his respective leaders continued to operate as they had in the past.

During the acquisition phase, Janice found that the Regional VPs were not receptive to her recommendations for a new color scheme and furnishings for all stores. As they were accustomed to making these decisions and were unaware of the change in policy, they resisted Janice's suggestions. Janice took the initiative to explain that the merged company was adopting Cyclone's existing model of roles and responsibilities—specifically, that all such decisions had been centralized.

By not making the Soccer Unlimited Regional VPs aware of this policy, their lack of understanding created delays in the rebranding. Their confusion over accountability and the numerous discussions between Janice and the new-to-the-company regional VPs to resolve this issue cost hundreds of thousands of dollars in wasted time and effort. This would have been avoided had the CEO broadly communicated his decision and the rationale early on.

The knowledge vacuum and the ensuing discussions to resolve the ambiguity drew the executives' attention and focus away from more important priorities during the transition to a new brand, such as customer satisfaction and their employee engagement levels. Had the CEO clearly communicated responsibilities and decision making much earlier, these delays could have been avoided. The Soccer Unlimited VPs may still have resisted what they perceived as a loss of authority and empowerment, but in the interim, the rebranding would have proceeded on time and on budget.

*As a leader*, identify and communicate early about:

*Change-related decisions*

- Who makes them?
- Which ones are outstanding and when will they be made?

- Which are made independently and which involve others?
- Who has the authority to make which ones?

*Implementation plan*

- Who stays in existing roles? Who changes roles?
- What responsibilities change?
- When do the changes come into effect?

### 3. Expected Behavior—Define and Govern Accordingly

The most successful change initiatives have a defined sponsor. The best sponsors are courageous leaders who rapidly address resistance. Resistance behavior can emerge as people seek clarity during times of uncertainty. You can alleviate some of this resistance by clearly defining expectations. Be as specific as possible. With anyone who is not meeting your expectations, get to it quickly as this is the evidence of uncertainty and possible resistance. This demonstrates accountability. Reward and celebrate desired behavior whenever possible. Remember that others' eyes are on you, noting how you are negotiating push-back in the change effort.

To achieve the newly desired state, change efforts typically require modifications to the corporate culture, behaviors, and norms. This is best achieved when group leaders and senior management model the desired behaviors that contribute to the change implementation plan. These behaviors are transparency, accountability, and collaboration.

Transparency

Leaders demonstrate this quality when they openly share information rather than holding back in a misguided belief that knowledge is power. Depending on the nature and scope of the change, decisions will be made at varying velocities. For example, with a bank merger, approvals must be sought from a variety of regulatory bodies, including the Competition Bureau, perhaps major shareholders, and others. As a result, some decisions cannot be made until such approvals are complete. To contrast, in the case of an outsourcing effort, the internal sponsor will make decisions. Decisions occur more rapidly and communication should quickly follow. When decisions are delayed or are dependent upon other factors, transparent leaders readily communicate decisions and advise when later decisions will be made.

Accountability

I can always tell fairly quickly when an organization lacks accountability. In these companies, I hear phrases such as:

"He's not met his objectives for 3 or 4 years, but he's not that bad. Besides, it's tough to recruit in this market."

"I'm not pushing myself so hard any more. My colleagues in the northwest region haven't delivered for the last several months and it doesn't seem to matter."

Conversely, in a culture of accountability, leaders follow up regularly to ensure their employees are meeting performance expectations. When they see members of their team not supporting or enabling the change, they have candid conversations and set the expectation that staff support the initiative. Then they check in later to confirm that the staff member followed through.

Collaboration

Collaborative leaders support the change effort. They meet all deadlines, even if they do not fully support the *rationale* for the change. If they have concerns, they voice them along with data to support their comments. As well, they consider what is best for the company and all stakeholders, valuing this over what is best for their particular area of responsibility.

"Susan", the VP, Manufacturing for a food services company, was responsible for facilities across the American Midwest. The company's oldest and largest manufacturing facility was situated on the edge of Chicago. With the passage of time, the surrounding region became a gentrified residential area. When Susan announced the decision to relocate the facility to a lower-cost location, many staff complained. It would be less convenient for them to get to work, even though they could use public transit to reach the new location. Within a few weeks, Susan realized that Frank, one of her general managers, was actively commiserating with plant employees and complaining about the decision. He had been saying that Susan and other executives cared more about profits than they did about the employees.

Susan quickly addressed this with Frank. Over the course of six weeks she had two face-to-face meetings with him. She outlined the benefits to customers and shareholders, and also:

- Reinforced the rationale for the change:
  - access to a highly skilled workforce
  - proximity to public transit
  - much lower taxes
- Pointed out the benefits to employees:
  - free parking
  - on-site fitness facility and child care
  - accessibility to transit
  - more windows and natural light
  - a well-stocked cafeteria

Furthermore, she specified what was expected from him—that he speak positively about the change inside and outside of the organization; that he share the rationale with his employees; and, that he do everything possible to contribute to a successful move. She was also clear that should Frank not behave as expected, he would no longer remain in a leadership role, and, in fact, may not remain with the organization at all.

Such clear expectations and holding people to account are the hallmarks of effective change leadership. Susan rapidly responded to employees' concerns. She did not take over Frank's leadership responsibilities, but provided him with more information so that he could communicate to his team. She set clear expectations for him, defined the expected leadership behaviors, and invested regular time to coach him on how to follow through. By modeling all these effective management behaviors, Susan acted as a role model for Frank that he could draw on when dealing with his own team.

In coaching Susan, I advised her to communicate the benefits and seek concerns from her leaders earlier in projects. Had she met with Frank and her other general managers earlier, she would have avoided the escalation of anxiety. She would also have been able to bring her leaders onside with fewer meetings, which would have been much more efficient.

### 4. Monitor: Follow Up

Successfully managing change requires leaders to pay attention to whether or not the company or department is achieving the desired results. One of the biggest impediments to achieving the ROI from a change effort is when new processes are not adopted as planned. With virtually every change effort, improving existing processes by introducing greater consistency delivers some of the greatest benefits.

Common benefits of organizational change efforts include:

- reduced expenses
- greater revenue
- increased market share
- better access to data
- improved accuracy of data
- improved health and safety
- better regulatory reporting

If you are the sponsor of the change effort, you will be well aware of the anticipated benefits. Should you be on the steering committee, and thus participating in guiding decisions and implementation, ensure you fully understand the expected benefits. If your division or department will be affected or if your staff will be required to change any of their practices, it is important you understand the rationale and the benefits. You will want to communicate these to your staff. Perhaps you are a recipient of the change or on the sidelines, as your division or team is not affected. It is still useful for you to understand the rationale so that you can support it—part of being a collaborative leader. It is not as important that you understand the benefits, however.

Whenever your team is expected to change their practices and processes, governance is key. Effective governance practices include monitoring peoples' activities to confirm that the changes have been made. The passage of time seems to be negatively correlated with adherence to change. Sometimes staff will adopt the new practices early on when they are being monitored, and when there is a high level of enthusiasm for the change. At this stage, there is typically a project management structure and oversight to the change efforts.

Remission

Six and nine months after the change has been completed and the formal project is dissolved, however, it is common for people to revert to the way they used to do things. They develop their own work-arounds. This can include creating duplicate processes, such as using excel spreadsheets to record and track their own data in addition to, or instead of, using the information provided through the new ERP system. In this example, duplicate sources of data may not match and decisions may be made using the incorrect data. As well, the duplicate activity is a labor cost that should not occur with the implementation of the ERP.

It can be very effective to assign individuals at various levels in the affected departments (which may be all departments or divisions in some cases) to shadow work processes at six, nine, twelve, and eighteen months postchange to identify what new procedures may have been missed and to identify any duplication.

Successfully monitoring the change process

> A large oil company implemented a new ERP with the significant benefit of capturing all discretionary expenses. This allowed the senior leadership to review expenses for travel, telecommunications, training and development, conferences, and other expenses in multiple ways—in aggregate, by division and department, and by supplier. A final significant benefit of adhering to the new system was that senior staff had greater transparency on expenses. This allowed them to more easily monitor year-over-year spending increases. As well, they could compare discretionary spending for one department over another and monitor trends.

*(continued)*

> The new ERP system also meant they could monitor when managers were not complying with company procedures, such as by purchasing goods or services from firms other than the identified set of preferred suppliers. As the supply chain group negotiated volume pricing with preferred suppliers, when managers purchased goods or services from other suppliers, it often cost the company more. Furthermore, this practice jeopardized the discount pricing from the preferred suppliers.
>
> The new system was met with some resistance because it interfered with the immediacy of a handwritten check. Entering the payment request through the new ERP system meant a three- or four-day turnaround and, because of this, some managers and executives did not immediately comply with the new process. However, if anyone bypassed the new system and generated a check by hand (for paying suppliers or others) the accounting department flagged the expense for review.
>
> How did the oil company address the lack of compliance to the new processes? For the first three occurrences by any given manager or executive, they followed up and reminded them of the new process and offered assistance. With the fourth violation, the accounting department escalated it to the manager or vice president's supervisor. The CEO received a report identifying any individual who circumvented the process seven or more times. She personally took action in these situations by speaking to the responsible executive member of his team.

While it was somewhat onerous for executives to follow up on the exceptions, the CEO recognized the benefits of sustained governance and modeling accountable leadership. She had led acquisitions at previous companies and learned the importance of careful oversight. In addition to the payment process noted above, employees identified sixty-four other processes as key enterprise processes for the oil company. Designated process owners monitored compliance to each of these sixty-four processes and lack of compliance was escalated. The CEO and executive leadership team ensured that all managers and supervisors understood the rationale for change, as we covered in Step 1. If employees actively resisted on continual basis, leaders were expected to take action, up to and including terminating the employee.

## 5. Incorporate your learnings

We know we can learn as much from our mistakes and disappointments as we can from our successes. However, it is not always obvious how to do this.

---

### Exercise #1 – Learning from the Past

Conduct an inventory of your last change process:

- What role did you play—sponsor, leader, contributor, recipient?
- Did you achieve your desired outcomes?
- Eighteen and twenty-four months later: did your employees adopt the expected and required changes to fully achieve the benefits?
- Did you overlook or minimize any of the steps in this THRIVE© model?
- Looking back, what might you have done differently?
- Looking ahead, what will be new? Identify at least one strategy.
- Who will you share your insights with—recognizing successful change is achieved by collaborating?

---

### Successful Change is Achievable

Change is a constant in our organizations today. It knows no bounds: no industry or geography is exempt. This is positive, as change is the hallmark of innovation as I have noted. Too many change efforts fail unnecessarily for many of the reasons I have pointed here, leaving employees frustrated and leaders disillusioned and seeking answers. It does not have to be this way! The historical benchmark of seventy percent unsuccessful change efforts, noted at the outset of this chapter, can indeed be improved.

By following the THRIVE© model with every change process, your track record will improve. At the same time, you will create cultural norms in the company that significantly reverse the tendency toward unsuccessful change outcomes; you set an example for others. Leaders and employees will expect and adapt to change more quickly. Increased employee engagement, customer satisfaction, and financial results will be your reward.

# CHAPTER 9

# Elevating Results through Innovation

## Innovation Is the Only Lasting Differentiator

Once strong companies and household names—Bethlehem Steel, Enron, Swissair, Commodore Computers, Polaroid, Atkins Nutritionals, Washington Mutual Bank, Bre-X Minerals, and Woolworths are no more. What differentiates the companies and brands that endure through economic cycles and changes in leadership? The enduring companies outlast their competitors through repeated transformation and innovation.

*Key Components of Innovation*

Boston Consulting Group (BCG) publishes a list, annually, of the most innovative companies across the globe. Those repeatedly identified as innovators include 3M, Amazon, Toyota, HP, Apple, GE, Google, and Proctor and Gamble. In this chapter, we will explore how you, as a leader, can fan the coals of innovation.

BCG attributes innovation to speed, lean R&D processes, leveraging technology, and systemically exploring adjacent markets. This is consistent with my experience. Let us explore each of these factors:

Speed

Speed really does matter. Forty-two percent of those reporting a culture of speed also rated their innovative capabilities as strong. Conversely, less than ten percent of slow cultures identified themselves as innovative.

Also, over forty percent identified long development times as an obstacle to innovation (BCG 2015 survey).

*Take action*

One of the quickest paths to creating a culture of innovation is to adopt a *bias for yes*. A rewarding side benefit of this is that it also heightens employee engagement. When you adopt a bias for yes, employee suggestions are adopted *quickly* and whenever possible. Later in this chapter, we will explore methods to capture employee ideas in systematic ways. However, do not overthink or overengineer this concept. Some of my clients have made huge strides by simply publicly committing to say "yes" to three ideas each month. With this level of transparency, they can ask others to hold them accountable to their commitment.

Lean R&D processes

Lean practices have moved from the sphere of manufacturing into many industries. TD Bank, with a long history of innovation in financial services, adopted lean practices early in the twentieth century. Innovative companies now apply these same principles to research and development.

*Take action*

If you have already applied Lean or other systems thinking to your processes, consider how you could extend this to your product development or R&D. If you have not yet applied systematic thinking to improving efficiency and reducing waste in your operations or production, it is time to do so.

Leveraging technology

In BCG's 2015 survey, exploiting technology platforms was identified as having the highest impact on innovation over the medium term. This is easiest for companies like Facebook and Amazon that were built upon a platform at their inception. It is, however, possible for every company. To ensure commitment to using a single platform, companies such as IBM, Amazon, and others have incorporated the use of big data and technology platforms into their innovation strategies.

The ubiquitous nature of technology has forever changed the role of the Information Technology department and the CIO. Employees in other departments across the company expect functionality, flexibility, and speed consistent with what they experience in their cars and from their smart phone apps and tablets.

Technology companies have had an advantage in this area. At Google, HP, IBM, and Netflix, for example, it has long been expected that everyone can and will participate in the development and leverage of technology. In financial services and retail, where accountability has been centralized with the CIO and IT departments, it has been a slower transition that started post-2005. These businesses are highly reliant on technology to mine information about customer behavior and to operate their core businesses; this drove changes to the traditional organizational structure and centralized control. Industries such as traditional manufacturing companies, utilities, and oil and gas have been the slowest to change. As a result, they have not innovated as quickly as other industries. Technology is foundational to best utilize customer information, foreign exchange processing, and so on, but authorization for technology choices and utilization largely remained with the CIO.

*Take action*
As leveraging technology is so fundamental to innovation, bring together your leadership team and discuss the following to determine your priority actions.

- Where is your organization on the continuum—close to the leaders of the pack like Amazon and IBM? In the middle like many banks and insurance companies? Or are you lagging?
- Do you have a technology strategy or innovation strategy? If not, it is time to create one. If so, ensure that you have incorporated the four attributes and actions identified in this section.

- Do you have a technology platform? If so, are you leveraging it or do you have an assortment of operating systems?
- Do you have a strategy for capturing and exploiting big data?
- Have you struck an appropriate balance between governing the selection and use of technology (the role of the CIO) to mitigate risks of cyber-security and maximizing efficiency and the customer experience by involving other parts of the company in selecting and utilizing technology?

Reviewing these questions will help you identify your gaps and establish your priorities. This is an area in which you will benefit from engaging external expertise.

Systematically exploring adjacent markets

The final crucial attribute of the most innovative companies is that they consistently explore adjacent markets. Growth never follows a hockey stick trajectory forever. If you are in a mature industry, as most of you are, you have many competitors and innovation in your existing market has slowed.

> Salesforce provides customer relationship management (CRM) services across the globe. Their customers include Bombardier (aerospace and transportation), Aldo (shoe retailer), and TELUS (telecommunications). In 2015, Salesforce announced an entrée into health care. To achieve this, they partnered with Phillips to create a cloud-based health care platform. Leveraging their strengths and core business in CRM, they sought out an adjacent market.

*Take action*
- Which new markets would benefit from your core capabilities, products, and/or services?
- How could you apply the principles of speed, Lean R&D, and leveraging your technology platform?

Richard Scott is the President and CEO of All Weather Windows. Recognized as an innovative leader, I asked Richard for his insights. When fostering innovation, Richard states the importance of understanding the difference between new features, which he defines as novelties, and innovation. "Innovation is something completely new to the industry, such as introducing an entirely new product or service to the consumers."

Richard says that fostering innovation requires leaders to: (1) start with your "why"; (2) identify your customers' problems, and (3) create a work environment in which no ideas are wrong."

After you confirm why you do what you do and/or why you need to change, then you can best determine what to change and how. When you identify problems facing your customers, you do not need to create the need for your new product or service; you fill the gap.

Encourage ideas. Build on ideas. The first or second idea might not be the ideal solution, but they generate more and more ideas. "Celebrate the failures. People will keep generating new ideas," says Richard.

Look for disruptors in the world around you. They need not be in your industry. These can include a new political party in power, economic changes resulting from the supply of oil and gas, or the popularity of Tesla's Model 3. What is changing and what opportunity does that create for your business? Always look to be a disruptor in your industry and be willing to be early adopters.

## Employee Engagement Is a Road Paved with Gold

We have a quiet killer of productivity, profitability, and innovation. Every day, close to one hundred million employees across North America arrive home at the end of their workday and complain about their boss. Staggering isn't it? These disengaged people work in every industry and at all levels. Their disenchantment represents a massive opportunity cost for companies. The impact to the North American economy is greater than that of unemployment. Sixty percent of engaged employees intend to remain at their place of employment, whereas seventy-five percent of disengaged employees are considering leaving. Astute corporate directors have identified this risk and are seeking reporting as part of their governance activities.

## Signs of Disengagement

- High or increased turnover
- Disproportionate turnover of employees with less than five-year tenure
- Decline in or low productivity
- Lack of new ideas and innovation—particularly from field and frontline people
- Low scores on employee engagement surveys
- Decline in customer satisfaction scores
- Declining service levels or product quality
- Leaders behaving in ways that are misaligned to the espoused corporate values
- Leaders not holding themselves or others accountable to commitments
- Leaders not addressing poor performance
- No visible succession planning and career progression opportunities

Contributors to employee disengagement are often unwitting or unconscious. Sometimes, corporate values have evolved and long-tenured leaders may not have adjusted their behavior accordingly. This can represent itself as: leaders believing that knowledge is power and not sharing information openly with employees; managers not supporting employee development and saying instead, "I had to pay my dues and put in my time; you do too"; when suggestions and ideas are resisted and/or discouraged; or through bullying and aggressive behavior.

The great news is that once you identify and address the sources of disengagement, you will increase mid- and long-term profitability while fostering a culture of innovation.

## Recommended Actions

- Employee orientation
- The "brown paper exercise"
- Employee focus groups

- Exit interviews
- Customer focus groups
- Evaluate succession planning and talent management practices
- Define and govern leadership competencies
- Objectively assess performance management practices

Let us explore each of these.

Employee Orientation

Many companies offer orientation for new employees. It is often led by HR and typically includes an overview of benefit programs, health and safety practices, and other useful information. In addition, there is a unique and highly beneficial practice that innovative companies may utilize.

When the person joins the organization, their leader asks them to observe and question virtually everything for the next six weeks to three months. It is not advisable that the person literally questions everything, but rather that they note their questions, their observations, and their ideas for this initial time period. Astute leaders realize that this initial phase is a fodder for creativity that will not be repeated. The person is seeing everything for the first time and with a fresh set of eyes. Once they have been with the organization for even six months, they will have acclimated to the organizational norms and culture and will not be flooded with ideas in the same way. The employee is asked to present a summary of observations, questions, and recommendations to their leader or the executive team at the end of ninety days or as soon as six weeks after joining the company.

In large or geographically dispersed companies, this is also a useful exercise when someone moves from one division or geography to another. It can be surprising how differently one division or region operates from another. In some instances, mitigating these differences and adopting more common practices can have multiple benefits including reduction in training expenses, higher quality product and/or services, and heightened profitability.

Brown Paper Exercise

As a picture paints a thousand words, so does the "brown paper exercise." Conduct this simple and powerful exercise by doing the following. Bring together a diverse group of employees. Ensure the group includes one or more people who interact with customers, one or more from operations, and one or more from administrative functions. The group will benefit from different demographics, varying years of service in the industry or company, people from different geographies or divisions, technical roles, and marketing or product roles, and so on.

Identify or ask the group to pick two to five processes that commence with a request from a customer. The customer request can originate in any way: call center, face-to-face, online through the web, telephone, RFP, and others. The processes can include customer complaint resolution, product or service order and delivery, customer inquiries, and so on.

Let's use an example. A construction firm may choose the process of responding to an RFP/bid for work, through preparation of the proposal and response. They could also use the process of completing the work including assignment of resources, undertaking the work through to invoicing the customer. They could also split this into two components and conduct a review of the invoicing process starting with the receipt of information from the field to preparation of invoice, to follow up when accounts receivable are late, and so on.

Utilize a roll of boardwalk style brown paper. You will need a room that is large enough to hang the paper across an expanse of wall or table space.

Ask the group to outline/draw the process from the customer interaction through to fulfillment.

Ideally, different people will participate in outlining various stages of the process. It need not be in intricate detail. It will be at the discretion *and* judgment of the group but should include enough detail to provoke questions, but not so much detail that you cannot fit the process onto six feet or so of brown paper.

Here is where this becomes really powerful.

Eliminate

The group should look at the process through this lens . . . "If I was the customer or client and I am paying for your product or services, what steps in your process would I tell you I do not want to pay for and/or I do not see value in receiving?"

I have seen teams identify the following as extraneous: paper statements mailed to clients; producing multiple photocopies so that different departments have a copy for reference; and hard-copy reports produced and distributed to clients at the completion of projects. Quite often, the group will identify duplicate and redundant processes, completed by different parts of the company at different stages in the process.

Simplify

Then have the group identify steps that can be automated or otherwise improved.

Stimulate Creativity

Finally, the group identifies enhancements that would benefit customers, shareholders, or employees. In some cases, these ideas may require further research and cost–benefit analyses.

Allow two to three hours to review each process. Some groups may think they need longer and that their business is more complicated than the norm. This is simply not the case—from banks to emergency rooms, a group will generate as many or more creative ideas when they have a limited time to do so.

Implement

This is where you hold your own feet to the fire. Wherever possible, implement the ideas generated by the group, particularly those that eliminate or simplify. In doing so, you stimulate a culture of innovation and employee engagement. It will be a wasted exercise if executives or middle management resist the changes and provide rationale, read excuses, for not making at least some of the recommended changes. If this happens, you will experience the immediate opportunity cost as well as the sustained loss of belief and initiative on the part of your employees.

### Employee Focus Groups

As with the brown paper exercise, assemble a diverse group of employees. Start by providing them with an intractable or expensive issue and ask them to collectively identify solutions or to identify one to two problematic processes or issues they would like to positively impact.

Ask someone to facilitate the discussion. You can use an in-house person who is well respected and can effectively engage with all personalities or an external expert. Spend two to three hours to brainstorm ideas and to gather consensus on a course of action or actions.

### Exit Interviews

The information acquired through exit interviews can be very useful in identifying patterns or systemic issues. The benefits from exit interviews are only realized when you do something with the information. If you are willing to make the changes you believe are warranted, then by all means conduct exit interviews and communicate broadly to your employees. Tell them, "the changes we are making are based on employee feedback. We are open to your suggestions so please continue to tell us what you think." If you are not willing to make the appropriate and realistic changes, do not invest resources in conducting exit interviews.

In some companies, employee turnover is highest in the first five years. This is potentially a sign of systemic disengagement. In my experience, this most often occurs when employees believe they are not receiving developmental opportunities and, therefore, will be unable to achieve their desired career goals. Employees self-select to leave an organization when they believe they are at risk of having invested too much time in that company without the career growth or satisfaction they had hoped for. In these situations, or when you are experiencing increased turnover or overall high levels of turnover, exit interviews can provide valuable insights.

### Customer Focus Groups

Your clients can be a wealth of knowledge and incite innovation. Customer focus groups are a great source of information and can also incent customer loyalty. The focus group can be led by one of your leaders if you have someone who can be highly objective, nondefensive, and is effective in leading a group discussion. You may also wish to utilize an external facilitator. To hold a successful focus group:

- Identify a representative sample of customers and invite them to participate.
- Form groups of six to eight customers. You may wish to hold three or four customer focus group meetings to ensure you capture a broad range of feedback.
- Gather their collective feedback, particularly identifying common themes.
- Develop action plans.

The following is a very highly effective tweak to customer focus groups that I have participated in. Rather than holding the focus group independently, *include your executive or leadership team.* Obtain permission from the participants to involve the company leadership. Utilize a skilled external facilitator (important in this case). Conduct the focus group meeting in a room that is large enough for the executive team to observe from a distance. This ensures that the observers do not distract the participants and the observers can follow the dialogue. Use microphones if necessary. The observers can take notes but must remain silent—no asking questions or seeking clarification. That will come later. In the meantime, the leaders will acquire valuable perspective about their company and its performance.

Plan sufficient time to enable the executives to meet with and thank the customers/participants after the meeting. In my experience, the leaders are highly motivated to share their business cards, address customer concerns, and seek additional feedback. Everyone wins. This technique can be particularly effective when your leaders are resisting what they may be hearing from customer surveys or from employees.

Succession planning, leadership competencies, and performance management practices are covered off in other chapters.

Your employees can be the greatest agents of innovation. If they have worked in other companies or industries, they have experienced successful interventions and some practices that will be applicable to your company. If they have spent their entire career in your company, they have a wealth of knowledge of what works well and where the stumbling blocks are. They may have been discouraged from sharing their ideas in the past, but it is never too late.

Re-engaging your workforce delivers positive results to the bottom line. Benefits include improved financial metrics, more highly satisfied customers, an improved health and safety record, and employee retention. Develop and implement a plan of action. You will reap short- and long-term benefits as you increase productivity and innovation while retaining and attracting superior talent.

## The Power of Innovation

As a frequent international traveler, I am a raving fan of Nexus (Canada) and Global Entry (United States). As a registered "trusted traveler," my passage through customs is expedited at many airports. There is an interesting back-story to Nexus.

> Let us cast our eyes back to 1998. These are the days before online check-in and predate airline kiosks. The airport is the second busiest in the country, serving tens of millions of passengers. The international terminal is very active in both departure and arrivals areas
>
> On the departures level, there are lengthy line-ups at airline counters. The previous week, the board approved a significant capital investment. The project will add twenty percent more airline counter capacity. One of the airport executives is scanning the terminal. He recently joined the company and is investing most of his first weeks in asking questions and observing. He sees the long line-ups and some impatient customers. He notices the hard-working airline staff but also notes that several of the airline counters are not manned with agents. He wonders if the expansion of airline counters will deliver the expected ROI. He thinks it may offer only short-term improvements as the metropolitan area grows and passenger traffic increases. He also recognizes that the low-margin airline business is unlikely to staff up sufficiently to man the increased counters. In fact, he realizes, even more, empty airline counters may result in increased dissatisfaction among passengers. He believes there is a better solution. He is not yet sure what that is.

He asks the executive team to delay announcing or commencing the capital renovations for one month while he undertakes further research. Within a few weeks, he has a groundbreaking idea. Using bank automated teller machines (ATMs) as an example, he recommends the development of self-serve kiosks for airline check-in and ticketing. Building on the functionality that allows customers to use a single kiosk to access any number of banks, he creates a vision of a multiairline check-in kiosk. The expansion of airline counters was shelved and replaced with a technology project to install what has now become commonplace in airports around the world.

A word on accountability from Walter Kresic, Vice President of Pipeline Integrity for Enbridge—"your right hand man/woman, your direct team and the people who report to them. . . this has to be at the centre of your desk all the time. Spend 50% of your time considering the team. Look at your team and understand them and what makes them tick. Spend time engaging on that subject a lot. 'Let's talk about why you are not fixing the process; let's not talk about the process. We are giving you everything you need; how can you be more innovative? What is stopping you from being innovative?' This can be frustrating sometimes, but it will free you. People enjoy these discussions. Then it is simply a matter of translating it to business results."

Repeated innovation is the only lasting differentiator. It can result from engaging your employee and customers. It results from a bias for yes. Speed, lean R&D, leveraging technology, and systematically exploring adjacent markets will fuel the innovation bonfire.

# Index

Accountability
 building blocks of, 4–5
 change and, 124
 creating a plan for, 94, 100
 culture of, 1–6
 establishment, 6
 factors undermining, 2–3
 lack of, 2–3
 roles and, 120
 sustained management of, 5
 workplace evaluation, 2
Accreditations, 71
Adjacent markets, exploring, 134–135
Alcoholics Anonymous, 23
Alignment, generating power through, 87–89
Alternate work option, consideration, 13–14
Amazon, 131
Annual performance setting, 93
Apple, 131
Assessment, 55–57

Backman, Cathy, 7–9
Behavioral gaps, 95
Boston Consulting Group (BCG), 131
Brevity of communication, 35–37
Brown paper exercise, 137–138
Business Analyst, 71
Butow, Eric, 41

Cadbury, 27
Career. *See also* Turning points, career
 alternate work option, consideration, 13–14
 change, consideration, 42
 compressed workweek, 12
 demanding roles, 9
 establishment of (without sacrificing a life), 7–26
 full-time work, 9
 healthy support network, 23–24

 leadership athleticism development, 16–23
 and life planning, 93
 options, 14–15
 part-time work, 11–12
 present situation, 14
 request for approval, 15–16
 satellite offices, 12–13
 telecommuting, 12
 work models, encouragement and accommodation of, 16
Change
 achievability and, 129
 benefits of efforts, 126
 expected behavior, 123–126
 factors influencing, 116–118
 follow up, 126–128
 incorporation of learnings, 129
 innovation and, 129
 internal and external factors, 116
 leading, 117–118
 monitoring the process, 127–128
 rationale for, 118–120
 remission, 127
 roles and responsibilities, 120–123
 THRIVE© model, 118–129
 urgency, 116–117
Clarity, providing, 90
Coaching, 80–81
 meeting, 93
Coates, John, 28
Collaboration, 124–126
Compensation, 87, 113
Compressed workweek, 12
Consequences, 5
Consultation/advice, 103
Courageous leadership, 28–30
 assessment, 48–49
Covey, Stephen, 24
Creativity
 fostering, 79–80
 stimulating, 139
Customer focus groups, 140–142

# INDEX

Data gathering, 57–59
Demanding roles, with spouse, 9
Demeanor, 31, 46
Disengagement, signs of, 136
80/20 rule, 76

Employee disengagement, 136
Employee engagement, 1, 135–142
Employee focus groups, 140
Employee orientation, 137
Employee performance, expectations, 112
Enbridge, 82
Energy management, 21
Enterprise Resource Planning (ERP) systems, 115, 120–121
Executive presence, 30–32
  assessment, 46–47
  character, 32
  physical presence, 31, 46
  style, 31
Executive programs, 71–72
Exit interviews, 140
Expectations
  managing, 110–111
  performance, 112
Exxon Valdez oil spill, 37

Feedback, providing, 99
Ferriss, Tim, 73
Flexibility, 17
*4-Hour Work Week, The* (book), 73–74
Full-time work, 9
Functional performance gaps, 95

GE, 131
Gender differences, 39–40
Goodwill, 27
Google, 131, 133
Growth, through pain, 82–84

Healthy support network, 23–24
*How To Succeed in Business Using LinkedIn* (book), 41
HP, 131, 133

IBM, 133
Ideas, implementation of, 139

Improvement, opportunities for, 56–57
Innovation
  components of, 131–135
  elevating results through, 131–143
  employee engagement, 135–142
  exploring adjacent markets, 134–135
  lean R&D processes, 132
  leveraging technology, 132–134
  power of, 142–143
  speed, 131–132
International assignments, 64–65

Job search, 42
Job security, 62–63
Judgment, 37

Kennedy, Jackie Onassis, 46
Key performance indicators (KPIs), 16, 87
Kraft, 27

LEAD490 model, 51–64
  assessment, 55–57
  data gathering, 57–59
  legacy clarification, 52–55
  90-day plan, 59–62
Leadership athleticism
  development of, 16–23
  flexibility, 17
  mental acuity, 17–18
  methods, 18–23
  resilience, 17
  speed, 17
Leadership brand
  construction of, 27–49
  courageous leadership, 28–30
  executive presence, 30–32
  gender differences, 39–40
  judgment, 37
  power of brevity, 35–37
  reputation, recovering, 37–39
  social media, use of, 40–43
  visibility, 32–35
Leadership success, keys to, 84–86
Leading organizational change, 115–129

Lean R&D processes, 132
Learning, from the past, 129
Legacy clarification, 52–55
Leveraging technology, 132–134
LinkedIn, 41–42

McCain, Michael, 17
Mental acuity, 17–18
Mentoring, 81–82
Midyear review, 93
Moore, Jake, 32
Moore, Lorraine
  courageous leadership assessment, 48–49
  executive presence assessment, 46–47
  leadership athleticism development, 16–23
  map to success, 24–26
  network map, 44–45
Multifaceted leadership, 73–86

Netflix, 133
Network
  building, 42
  expanding, 35
Network map, building, 44–45
90-Day plan, 59–62
No pretend time off (PTO), 18–19

Opportunities, 113
Opportunity costs, 4, 87, 113, 135, 139
Options
  assessing, sabbaticals/leaves, 66–67
  work, 14–15
Organizational change. *See* Change
Orientation, employee, 137

Pareto's 80/20 rule, 76
Part-time work, 11–12
Payment, one-time, 114
Pearson, Michael, 101–102
People management, 84, 85
Performance
  activity level and, 112–113
  benefits of managing to, 91
  clarity, 90
  compensation and, 113
  expectations, 112
  factors for success, 91–92
  feedback, providing, 99
  generating power through alignment, 87–89
  harnessing, 87–100
  management process, 93
  poor performance
    acumen/knowledge and, 96
    casting out, 92, 95
    discussing, 97–98
    individual, 95
    team performance, 95–96
  reward and recognition, role, 89–90
  template for recording and reporting on measures and progress, 98
  tenure and, 112
Performance improvement plan, 93
Personal brand, 43
Physical health, 19
Physical presence, 31, 46
Plan, building, 14
Poor performance. *See* Performance, poor performance
Potential, performance and, 105, 110–111
Proctor and Gamble, 131
Productivity
  and creativity, 79–80
  harnessing, 74–79
  and organizational change, 120
Project Management Professional (PMP), 71
Projects, 1
Prosci (Change Management), 71

Reflection, 19–21
Remote work and telecommuting, 12
Reputational recovery, 37–39
Resilience, 17
Resistance, 123
Responsibilities, roles and, 120–123
Results, 4
Retirements, 103
Return on investment (ROI), 76

Reward and recognition programs, 89–90
Roadmap, building, 25–26

Sabbaticals, taking, 65–68
Salesforce, 134
Satellite offices, 12–13
Self awareness, 6
Self-management, 84, 85–86
Situational leadership, 5
Social media, leveraging, 40–43
Special payment, 114
Speed, 131–132
Starbucks, 40
Stretch roles, 108–109, 111
Substandard performance, 92
Success
  factors for, 91–92
  keys to, 84–86
  map to, 24–26
Succession crisis, overcoming, 101–105
  demographics, 102
  planning practices, 104–105
  retirements, 103
  successors, identifying, 101–102
Succession planning process
  assessing potential, 105
  considerations, 107–108
  consistency, 109
  development through stretch roles, 108–109
  expectations, managing, 110–111
  mobility, 107
  performance rating, 105
  review of, 107
  talent management and, 105–111
  timeframe, 105

Support networks, 23–24
Sustainment, 4–5

Talent management, 101–114
Task management, 84, 85
Tata Motors, 27
Taylor, Kathleen, 41
TD Bank, 22, 132
Technology, leverage of, 132–134
Telecommuting, 12
Tenure and performance, 112
3M, 131
THRIVE© (change) model, 118–129
Toyota, 37–38, 131
Transparency, 123–124
Trustworthiness, 38
Turning points, career
  external factors, 52
  internal factors, 52
  international assignments, 64–65
  LEAD490 model, 51–62
  playing it safe versus remaining challenged, 62–64
  pursuing further education, 68–72
  sabbaticals/leaves/absences, 65–68

Visibility
  generating opportunity through, 32–35

Weight Watchers, 23
Working models
  encouragement and accommodation of, 16
Work–life balance, 11

# OTHER TITLES IN THE HUMAN RESOURCE MANAGEMENT AND ORGANIZATIONAL BEHAVIOR COLLECTION

- *You're a Genius: Using Reflective Practice to Master the Craft of Leadership* by Steven S. Taylor
- *Competencies at Work: Providing a Common Language for Talent Management* by Enrique Washington and Bruce Griffiths
- *Manage Your Career: 10 Keys to Survival and Success When Interviewing and on the Job, Second Edition* by Vijay Sathe
- *On All Cylinders: The Entrepreneur's Handbook* by Ron Robinson
- *The Resilience Advantage: Stop Managing Stress and Find Your Resilience* by Richard S. Citrin and Alan Weiss
- *Marketing Your Value: 9 Steps to Navigate Your Career* by Michael Edmondson
- *Success: Theory and Practice* by Michael Edmondson
- *Leading The Positive Organization: Actions, Tools, and Processes* by Thomas N. Duening, Donald G. Gardner, Dustin Bluhm, Andrew J. Czaplewski, and Thomas Martin Key
- *Performance Leadership* by Karen Moustafa Leonard and Fatma Pakdil
- *The New Leader: Harnessing The Power of Creativity to Produce Change* by Renee Kosiarek
- *Employee LEAPS: Leveraging Engagement by Applying Positive Strategies* by Kevin E. Phillips

## Announcing the Business Expert Press Digital Library

*Concise e-books business students need for classroom and research*

This book can also be purchased in an e-book collection by your library as

- *a one-time purchase,*
- *that is owned forever,*
- *allows for simultaneous readers,*
- *has no restrictions on printing, and*
- *can be downloaded as PDFs from within the library community.*

Our digital library collections are a great solution to beat the rising cost of textbooks. E-books can be loaded into their course management systems or onto students' e-book readers. The **Business Expert Press** digital libraries are very affordable, with no obligation to buy in future years. For more information, please visit **www.businessexpertpress.com/librarians**. To set up a trial in the United States, please email **sales@businessexpertpress.com**.